ᵥᵢₙ𝅭EDGE

G000096262

Book of
WALKS

by George Longden

Silk Press Books

MMI

Published by The Silk Press
14a Bath Street, Hale, Cheshire WA14 2EJ
Telephone 0161 929 4884   Fax 0161 929 8656

ISBN 1-902685-08-3

Photographs: Matthew Stansfield, Paul Roberts
and George Longden
Illustrations and Maps: Joe Longden
and George Longden

Kath. 277432

LivingEDGE Book of Walks

page # Contents

Where the walks are located

The LivingEDGE map is illustrative rather than geographical!

Our route lies directly ahead here, but if you wish to look at the site of Engine Vein Mine, follow the track round to the left. Mining took place in and around the cleft surrounded by open ground a few hundred yards further on, on the right (**3. Alderley Edge Mines**).

Return to the bend in the track, and take the wide path on the left, which leads up to the open ground of Stormy Point. Beyond the open area, a path marked as suitable for wheelchairs swings sharply to the left. Follow this path, which eventually turns right and leads to a hillock on top of which a stone plinth marks the site of Alderley Edge beacon, which was shown on Saxton's 1577 map of Cheshire. From the early eighteenth century until 1931 a small rectangular windowless building stood on this site. A pointed roof was added in 1779. Walk down the other side of the beacon hill. At the corner of the boundary wall which is on your left, a path from the right is joined.

Walk on ahead along this path. Ignore the first path off to the right, but take the second (at a point where a field boundary fence can be seen above on the left). The path descends a little, and then continues beneath the outcropping rocks. Castle Rock, a hundred yards or so along the path, is said to have been the site chosen for a castle in the thirteenth century, but abandoned in favour of Beeston.

Just beyond Castle Rock, steps descend from the left. Carry straight on, below further outcrops, to the Wizard's Well. In the legend which was made much of (and elaborated) for the nineteenth-century excursionists, the wizard bought a passing farmer's white horse, and took the farmer deep inside the hill to show him the sleeping army of King Arthur for which the horse was needed. Note the inscription above the stone trough. Beyond the well, the path descends more steeply. Continue diagonally down the Edge, in a more or less straight line, following the best made paths. You will emerge at a track between houses, which leads on to Mottram Road (as do all the paths which lead to the bottom of the Edge). Turn left, and walk along Mottram Road back to Alderley Edge village.

1. ALDERLEY EDGE AND THE RAILWAY

Before the opening of the railway in 1842, what is now the main street of Alderley Edge was occupied only by three or four cottages and two farm houses, all of them antiquated thatched structures. The Manchester and Birmingham Railway Company placed a station here with two types of future passenger in mind: the commuter and the excursionist. The railway company encouraged the 'merchant princes' of Manchester to move out to Alderley Edge by offering free railway travel to Manchester for twenty one years for anyone who "erected a dwelling house of the annual value of at least £50 within one mile from Alderley station."

The Trafford family which owned the lower, western, slopes of

the hill, which fell within the township of Chorley in the parish of Wilmslow, quickly sold land for building. The higher parts of the Edge, which were in the parish of Alderley, belonged to the Stanley family which refused to sell. The Stanleys had planted the Edge with beech, fir and birch, and allowed public access once or twice a week. The new railway brought thousands of working class excursionists from Manchester at holiday times, though not all got far beyond the hotel erected by the railway company next to the station in 1844, or the de Trafford Arms, which was rebuilt on a larger scale in 1859. The excursionists seem not to have worried the Stanleys as much as the permanent invasion of the middle class commuters. Lady Stanley wrote to Lord Stanley: "The Manchester gentry are much more annoying to one's comfort and enjoyment, as one can neither handcuff nor great dog them if they are intrusive or offensive."

The Stanleys regarded the name Alderley as their own, and were outraged when it was adopted for the new settlement at the foot of the hill. The historian Fletcher Moss described what happened in 1863 when the second Lord Stanley was appointed Postmaster General: "He soon showed his authority and power by sending all letters directed to residents in the new Alderley to the dead letter office, or redirected to Chorley. I can well remember the confusion which was caused in the district by the new postal regulations..."

2. NETHER ALDERLEY

Nether Alderley corn mill, which presents little to the public view from the road but a long stone flagged roof and low doorway, looks ancient, and is. The structure is sixteenth century, making this one of the oldest as well as best preserved water mills. Corn was ground here commercially until 1939. After the war the mill was presented to the National Trust, and was restored by Dr Cyril Boucher and his sons. It is open to the public as a working museum on certain days between April and October. The machinery is mostly nineteenth century. Enclosed within the building are two overshot water wheels, with a total fall of twenty five feet, which drive two pairs of composite French grindstones.

The mill itself forms part of the dam across the valley which retains the mill pond. The old Alderley Hall was built in the early seventeenth century by the side of the pool. A moat was cut, leaving the house on an island. The Stanleys, lords of the manor of Alderley, lived here until 1779, when a recently built grand extension was destroyed by fire. The family then moved to a hall at the far end of the three hundred acre Alderley Park to the south.

Stanley associations are everywhere in the tiny village of Nether Alderley. Across the main road from the mill, and just beyond a narrow lane, is the former Eagle and Child coaching inn (named for the Stanley crest). At the bottom of the lane is St

Nether Alderley corn mill

Mary's church, full of Stanley memorials. The white Rectory is adjacent. The Stanleys appointed the Rector, of course. That office was occupied from 1805 to 1837 by the Reverend Edward Stanley, author of the 'Familiar History of English Birds', a man much devoted to his parish who extended the seventeenth-century Free School which can be seen at the gateway to the church.

3. ALDERLEY EDGE MINES

Within the sandstones of the Edge are deposits of copper and lead, and small quantities of many other ores, including silver and gold. The Alderley Edge mines are amongst the oldest in the country, having been worked since the early bronze age. Grooved stone hammer and axe heads of prehistoric appearance have been found on the Edge – they have in the past been used as doorstops in cottages and farms. In a book published in 1878, Dr J. D. Sainter described and illustrated a collection of stone tools recently discovered in old diggings "together with an oak shovel that had been very roughly used." Sainter suggested that the tools might be prehistoric, though this could not then be proved. The oak shovel disappeared from academic view until the author Alan Garner recognised from Sainter's illustration that the shovel used to hang on the wall of the Alderley Edge Council School which he had attended as an infant. Garner has described in a recent collection of essays (*The Voice That*

Thundered, Harvill Press, 1997) how he retrieved the shovel from junk crammed under the school stage, and how many years later, in 1993, radio carbon dating proved the shovel to be around 3,700 years old.

It is likely that the Romans also mined the Edge. In 1995 a hoard of Roman coins was found in an old shaft on Engine Vein. Written evidence of early modern workings is scanty, partly because of the 1779 fire at Alderley Old Hall, where the records would be kept. One of the earliest references occurs in the Cheshire Quarter Sessions records of 1696, when a dispute over the ownership of a mine led to the use of chains and a winch by which workmen underground "were in a very violent manner forced out of the mines." The main period of copper mining was in the 18th and 19th centuries. Most of the workings visible on the surface, and most of the shafts and galleries below, probably date from that time. LE

copper mine workings on Alderley Edge

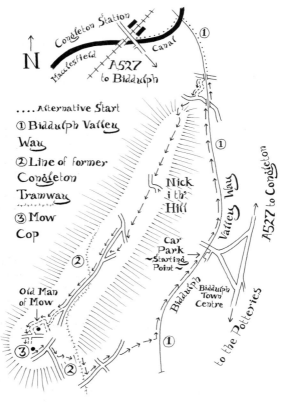

LivingEDGE Walk No. 2

Biddulph to Mow Cop

N

Congleton Station

Macclesfield

A527
to Biddulph

Canal

①

.... Alternative Start

① Biddulph Valley
Way

② Line of former
Congleton
Tramway

③ Mow
Cop

②

Old Man
of Mow

③

②

①

Nick
i th'
Hill

①

Valley Way

A527 to Congleton

Car
Park
~ Starting
Point ~

Biddulph

Biddulph
Town
Centre

to the Potteries

LENGTH OF WALK: Approximately six and a half miles (or eight and a half miles from the alternative starting point at Congleton Station).

DEGREE OF DIFFICULTY: Low / medium.

PUBLIC TRANSPORT: A bus service runs between Congleton and Biddulph. Congleton Station is on the railway line from Manchester to Stoke-on-Trent via Stockport and Macclesfield.

ORDNANCE SURVEY MAPS: At 1:25,000, the northern part of this walk can be found on Pathfinder map 776 (Congleton). The southern part is on Pathfinder map 792 (Kidsgrove and Leek).

This circular walk begins at the site of the railway station which used to serve the small North Staffordshire town of Biddulph. The disused railway has been converted into the Biddulph Valley Way. We walk down the pleasantly wooded line for two miles or so to Dane in Shaw on the outskirts of Congleton, before doubling back beside a brook, then climbing up to the long ridge of Congleton Edge. A rocky path follows the boundary between Staffordshire and Cheshire, above precipitous quarry faces.

An unavoidable stretch of road finishes the gentle climb to the strangely jumbled village of Mow Cop. From the famous folly in the form of a ruined castle magnificent views can be had on a fine day, across Cheshire to the hills of Lancashire, to Frodsham Hill, to Beeston and Wales beyond, and south into Shropshire, and across the sprawling expanse of the Potteries. We return to Biddulph mostly along field paths, following at one point the line of an early tramway, on which horses pulled coal trucks over the hill and down to Congleton.

ALTERNATIVE ROUTE: *You might want to start and end this walk at Congleton Station. This adds about two miles to the walk. From the station, go down the steps to the Macclesfield Canal. Turn left and walk east along the towpath (away from the overbridges). After half a mile, take the steps down to the Biddulph Valley Way. Turn right and walk to the first bridge over a road. At the steps on the right beyond the bridge you join the walk as described below – see * in the text. At the end of the walk described below you will need to continue down the Biddulph Valley Way to reach this point and return the same way to Congleton Station.*

The starting point for this walk is the car park on the site of the former Biddulph railway station. To reach this from the north by road, take the A527 from Congleton to Biddulph, but before coming to the centre of Biddulph, turn right directly in front of the Biddulph Arms Hotel into Halls Road. At the junction with a road coming up from Biddulph on the left, carry straight on for a few yards, then turn left into Smokies Way. **The Biddulph Valley Way (1)** car park is on the right.

From the car park, turn right onto the trail, which crosses the road. The first half mile is a bit scruffy, but you are soon in the countryside, descending gently through woods toward Congleton. You will see the A527 below on the right from time to time; eventually the road is crossed on a high bridge. About 500 yards further on, the trail crosses another road on a lower iron bridge. (*This is the point where the alternative route from Congleton Station joins the circular walk.)

Go down the steps on the left before the iron bridge. The Congleton-Leek road here crosses the Dane in Shaw Brook by the Higher Dane in Shaw Bridge. Mills lay downstream; evidence of water supply arrangements can be seen below the bridge.

Our route lies along the track on the left at the bottom of the steps down from the former railway. The track passes between the brook and a former Methodist chapel, and leads up to the Castle Inn, on the Congleton-Biddulph road.

Cross over the road (watch out for traffic coming round the blind corner on the right), walk to the right along the footpath for a few yards, then take the path on the left between gardens. This path climbs along the edges of small fields toward Congleton Edge. It is easily followed, and there are waymarkers on the stiles.

When the path reaches the crest of the lower part of the ridge, turn right and walk up to the top of the ridge. A stile leads into birch woods. The path is rocky and the bracken dense for about three quarters of a mile, but there are sweeping views to the right over the Cheshire Plain. Beware the steep quarry faces below the path on the right. The path descends slightly at Nick i th' Hill to a narrow road. Cross, and continue along Congleton Edge on the wider but still stony track (signed Pot Bank) beyond.

After half a mile the track ends at a road junction. Our route almost as far as Mow Cop now has to use the road (which can be quite busy at times) along the spine of the hill. The first stretch is narrow and has no verges. It can be avoided by walking for a few yards down the road on the left, then taking the well signed path on the right. This leads for a few hundred yards along the edge of a former quarry, before joining the road beyond a cottage. Turn left and continue along the ridge-top road. Rough verges on the right mean that for part of the way traffic can be avoided. About 500 yards further on the **Congleton Tramway (2)** joined the ridge-top from the right, having climbed diagonally up the hillside from Congleton Moss.

At Roe Park, a wide track entrance on the right, a waymarked path leads directly towards Mow Castle. This path is rough, overgrown and difficult to follow. It is probably better to continue along the road toward **Mow Cop (3)** for a few more hundred yards, over the brow ahead, and then take the waymarked track on the right, which is signed for Mow Cop Folly.

Follow the track between old smallholdings for a quarter of a mile to a junction of tracks. Turn right here (following the Staffordshire Way and Mow Cop Trail waymarkers) and follow the track over the crest of the ridge and round to the left. On the left is the Old Man of Mow, a pillar of stone which is said to have been left standing as the quarry face receded.

The track snakes round to join a quiet road. Turn right, then immediately left onto the track which leads to the Castle. From the turning circle in front of Beacon House, our route lies down to the right of the cottage and to the left of the hill on which the castle stands. But it is worth climbing the steps up to the folly itself, to enjoy the views.

Then take the path which zig-zags down, keeping Beacon House to your left. Note the old millstone quarries on the right. At the bottom, turn left below the hill with the cottage on top. After a few yards, take the path on the right, between the wall and the fence. Follow the path around the hillside, above houses. Where another path is joined, turn right, and walk down between bungalows to the road. Turn right, then left after the church.

Walk down the road for a few hundred yards. Opposite a telephone box, turn left onto a track, which becomes a field path. Walk through the fields, with the fence on your right. Where the fence turns right and is replaced by a hedge, follow. Keep the hedge on your right.

This path follows the line of the Congleton Tramway as it descends toward the site of Stone Trough Colliery. Beyond a stile, evidence of a later tramway can be seen, crossing the line of the Congleton Tramway. Coal was taken along this tramway, which passed through a tunnel under Mow Cop, to Kent Green on the Macclesfield Canal.

After the stile, continue straight on, down to the road. The Congleton Tramway continued toward the waste heaps further down the valley. We turn left on the usually quiet road. A ruined colliery engine house can be seen on the right. At the cross roads, continue ahead and walk down a holly-lined lane for about a quarter of a mile.

Take the signed field path on the right. Walk diagonally across the field to the fence on the left, then follow the fence, keeping it to your left. Over the stile, carry straight on with the hedge on your right. At the track beyond cottages, carry straight on. After a few hundred yards, the Biddulph Valley Way crosses the track on a low bridge. Walk up to the former railway, and turn left, crossing the bridge. The car park which was our starting point lies about half a mile ahead.

1. THE BIDDULPH VALLEY WAY

The Biddulph Valley Way utilises the northern section of the former Biddulph Valley line of the North Staffordshire Railway. This line enjoyed what has been described as *the queer distinction* of being opened three times *("Manifold": The North Staffordshire Railway, 1952)*.

The Biddulph Valley contained large reserves of coal. The name Biddulph means "by the diggings", though we don't know whether the Anglo-Saxons dug here for coal, stone, sand or clay. Access to the valley from nearby industrial areas was difficult. When the age of the steam railway dawned, the potential benefits of a line through the valley were obvious to the coal owners. The North Staffordshire Railway Company, however, drove its main line from Congleton to Stoke through Harecastle, not through Biddulph. The coal owners had to force the NSR into action by preparing to build an independent Biddulph line. This ploy was successful, and the NSR obtained an Act in 1854 which authorised the construction of a line from Brunswick Wharf in Congleton (with a spur to the main line) through the Biddulph valley and on to Stoke via Ford Green and Bucknall.

Building work did not begin until August 1858. The line was not complete when the parliamentary time limit expired on 3rd August 1859. To avoid fines, the line was "opened" for the first time on that day, though no trains ran. At a celebratory dinner, relief was expressed that the navvies working on the line had behaved so well. Perhaps this was due to the Biddulph schoolmaster, who had volunteered to instruct the navvies for an hour and a half every day.

In 1860 the line was opened for mineral traffic. This was, in the words of the historians of Biddulph, "perhaps the most important event in the history of the valley" (J. Kennedy (Ed): Biddulph.

1980). The coal and ironworks of Robert Heath-were rapidly expanded, and the town took its modern form.

It was not until 1864 that the line opened for passengers. The service was always a limited one, and it was discontinued in 1927. The warehouse and coal sidings at Biddulph Station (which was more accurately known as Gillow Heath until 1897) remained in use until 1964. The line north of Heath Junction closed completely in 1969.

2. CONGLETON TRAMWAY

In the eighteenth century coal was carried from the mines of the Biddulph Valley to the growing industrial town of Congleton either by packhorse over Congleton Edge, or by the rather indirect road which ran along the eastern side of the valley to join the Congleton-Leek road (the A527 route was not opened until the 1820s).

The Congleton Tramway was an early nineteenth century attempt to provide a cheaper route for coal from Stone Trough Colliery, which was one mile to the south east of Mow Cop village. The line climbed 180 feet up to the ridge at an average gradient of 1 in 26, then ran down the other side to Congleton Moss, dropping 550 feet at an average gradient of 1 in 20.

Much of the three and a half mile line is followed by public footpaths or roads today – our walk uses short stretches of the route.

Evidence of the tramway can be seen in the form of low embankments and shallow cuttings in fields, and the occasional stone sleeper can be found.

The tramway was evidently narrow gauge, and the waggons would be horse-drawn. J. C. Hopkins, the historian of the tramway, described in *Transport History* (1971) how he found one of the original rails at the site of the coal wharf at Moss Lane in Congleton in 1967. The cast iron rail was about three feet in length, and oval or egg-shaped in section.

This confirms what appears to be the only contemporary written reference to the line: J. C. Farey wrote that the tramway was "laid with oval bars of iron, on top of which the pulley-formed wheels of the trams ran" *(General View of the Agriculture of Derbyshire, Vol 3, 1817).*

Farey stated that the coal yard at the Congleton end of the line had been established in or around 1807, and he added "when I saw this railway in July 1809, it seemed to be quite disused, the reason of which I did not happen to hear." However, the coal wharf and the whole of the Cheshire part of the line are shown on Bryant's Cheshire map of 1831. It is likely that the opening of the Macclesfield Canal in that year led to the final closure of the Congleton Tramway.

3. MOW COP

The village of Mow Cop, which straddles the border between Cheshire and Staffordshire, is best known for its folly, Mow Cop Castle, which is itself bisected by the county boundary. The castle

was built by Randle Wilbraham in or around 1754, to serve as an "eyecatcher" on the skyline when viewed from Rode Hall, near Scholar Green in Cheshire. The castle is said to have been used by the Wilbrahams, and by the Staffordshire Sneyds, as a summerhouse, and to have been fitted with a roof, floors, glazed windows and a door. In the nineteenth century, a local tradition held that the roof of the folly had been constructed so that it could hold a warning beacon fire. By the twentieth century, the sham ruin was on the verge of becoming truly ruinous. It was repaired in the nick of time, and was taken over by the National Trust in 1937.

The gritstone around the folly was quarried for building stone, and for millstones. An account published in 1726 described how "they cleave [the millstones] from the rock with a great number of small wedges driven in with small strokes, lest the stone should crack or flaw." The marks left by this procedure can still be seen on the quarry faces.

By the early years of the nineteenth century Mow Cop was still sparsely settled; the only inhabitants were "a few quarrymen and grit sellers with their families, uncouth in manner, and unique in attire", according to a correspondent of the *Macclesfield Courier*, writing in 1856. The growth of collieries, ironworks and potteries nearby brought increasing numbers to the village.

Miners in particular were notorious for spending their supposedly high wages on drink and debauchery, but the growth of Mow Cop was accompanied by what the *Courier* writer called "a wonderful revolution in manners." The miners would now use their money to "buy and build their own freehold homes on sites at once cheap and convenient." The tastes and the sanitary condition of the people were improved by "the competition liberally encouraged by the principal employers by means of rewards for the neatest and best kept cottages."

The civilising of Mow Cop was partly the result of religious revivalism. Mow Cop's second claim to fame is as the birthplace of Primitive Methodism. A plaque by the car park to the south of the folly celebrates the original camp meeting on the hill in 1807, which was said to have been attended by 4,000 people. **LE**

Old Man of Mow

Bollington to Rainow

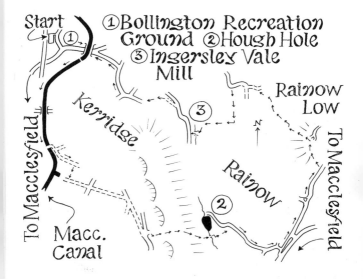

Start ①Bollington Recreation Ground ②Hough Hole ③Ingersley Vale Mill

Kerridge

Rainow Low

Rainow

To Macclesfield

To Macclesfield

Macc. Canal

②

③

LENGTH OF WALK: Approximately five and a half miles.

DEGREE OF DIFFICULTY: Moderate.

PUBLIC TRANSPORT: Bollington is served by buses from Macclesfield, and from Stockport via Poynton.

ORDNANCE SURVEY MAP: At 1:25000, this walk can be found on Pathfinder Map 759 (Macclesfield and Alderley Edge) or on Outdoor Leisure Map 24 (The Peak District – White Peak Area).

This walk begins in Bollington, a former cotton town in the deep valley of the River Dean, on the edge of the east Cheshire hills. We walk out along the Macclesfield Canal to Kerridge fields. Kerridge ridge is approached along the trackbed of an old quarry tramway. A path between quarries leads up to the top of the ridge. We drop down the other side to cross the upper Dean, here a tiny stream which nevertheless powered (at this point and higher) four cotton mills in the early industrial revolution. From Hough Hole quiet roads and field paths lead up to Rainow Low, a former quarrying and mining hamlet. We follow an old packhorse trail back toward the valley. Our route back to Bollington then passes behind Ingersley Hall, in front of the giant wheelhouse of Ingersley Vale Mill, and around the side of Kerridge hill on what may have been a Roman or even earlier way from the Cheshire plain into the hills of the Peak.

The walk begins at the Middlewood Way car park, Adlington Road, Bollington. Cross over Adlington Road from the car park, and enter the **Recreation Ground (1)** opposite. Walk through the "Rec" to the exit at the far right hand corner, above the tunnel which brings the River Dean through the rock of the valley wall to avoid the canal embankment and aqueduct.

Cross the road in front of the aqueduct, go through the "Hole i' th' Wall", and climb the steep steps. A gate provides access to the canal towpath. Turn right, and follow the canal away from the aqueduct. Walk along the towpath for about two-thirds of a mile, passing the Adelphi Mill (built as a cotton mill in 1856). At the next bridge, go up the steps, over the bridge, and follow the track round to the right and then straight on, into the fields.

Enter the field on the right through a gate in the wire fence. On the other side of the field, a stream is crossed by a plank. Walk through the next field, then turn left up the long straight trackway which heads toward Kerridge hill. This was the route of a tramway which brought stone from the Kerridge quarries to the canal. Cross over Clarke Lane, and walk up the incline past Endon House.

A very steep section of tramway continued ahead, passing under Victoria Bridge (built 1837). We turn right, and walk up the straight track to Windmill Lane. Cross over the road into the Endon Quarry entrance. The windmill, demolished in the 1940s, stood to the right. Take the path on the right at the end of the wooden fence, and follow it up to the top of Kerridge ridge.

Climb over the wall by the stile, and walk across to the edge of the hill. Rainow lies below.

From hereabouts, scurrilous 19th-century persons who had climbed up from Rainow under cover of darkness would broadcast scandal and insult as the villagers prepared for bed – until the miscreants' megaphone was found, hidden in an old mineshaft, and confiscated.

Walk down the steep hillside toward Rainow. The path is faint but should be discernible, veering a little to the right. Below a path which passes along the hillside at a lower level, walk straight down to the River Dean (little more than a stream, here) at the foot of the hill.

As we descend the hill, we get an aerial view of **Hough Hole (2)**, including the mill pool (the mill was at the far end), mill workers' cottages, and, higher up Sugar Lane, Hough Hole Farm and Hough Hole House.

Cross the Dean by the bridge, then cross the tributary stream by the stone slab on the right. Climb the stile in the wall, walk up the field to a gate, and walk on, with the fence on your left, to join Sugar Lane above Hough Hole House. Turn right and walk up Sugar Lane; at the point where a plantation of fir trees faces a row of old stone cottages, bear left into Chapel Lane. At the top, before the main road, turn left into narrow Stocks Lane. Past the village stocks, continue ahead, taking the lane to the left of the Robin Hood Inn.

After a few hundred yards, at a grass triangle, bear right.

Lowerhouse Mill, a small cotton mill built in 1792, was sited on the right. The quiet lane climbs up toward Big Low. After about 300 yards, take the waymarked path that begins at the far end of the barn beyond Back-of-the-Crofts, on the left. Follow the path through stiles around the hillside toward the hamlet of Rainowlow.

After the gate in front of the first houses, pass through the small gap in the wall on the left, climb down the steps, and walk straight on, climbing a stile into a wide walled green way, which soon narrows into what appears to be an old packhorse trail, perhaps used to bring stone and coal from the Rainowlow quarries and mines down toward the Cheshire plain.

Walk down to the stream in the clough below, ignoring the path which branches off to the left. The path joins a stream and follows it for a while, first to the right, then to the left, then to the right again, where a track is joined. Bear left; beyond a gate, turn right on a stone-surfaced road.

At the corner beyond Oakenbank Cottages, take the path on the left, which is waymarked as part of the Gritstone Trail. Beware the steps - they may be slippery. The path follows the boundary wall of the grounds of Ingersley Hall, which was built in 1775 by John Gaskell, and extended in 1833. The Gaskell family bred horses here in the nineteenth century: hence the extensive stabling.

Past the Hall and outbuildings, the wall and path make a right angle. Turn right, and walk down into the valley of the River Dean. Cross over the stone bridge, turn right on the track beyond, and walk past **Ingersley Vale Mill (3)**, passing under the iron trough which fed water from a hillside leat to a giant waterwheel. In the valley below Ingersley Vale Mill lay Rainow Mill, which was a cotton mill in the 19th century, a paper mill before that, and was possibly the site of Rainow's medieval corn mill.

The Rainow Mill pool has been filled in for use as a rough car park. A few yards further on, walk up the short muddy track on the left which leads up to a field path. This may have been part of a medieval and earlier route from the Cheshire Plain into the Peak District. Follow the path around the hillside. The industrial revolution town of Bollington is laid out below.

At the end of the field path, beyond a gate, Cow Lane leads down to Chancery Lane. Take the second road on the right, in front of the Red Lion, down into the village. At the bottom of the hill, turn left into Water Street, which leads to the canal aqueduct, past which lie the Recreation Ground and our starting point.

1. BOLLINGTON RECREATION GROUND

For a hundred years, the Recreation Ground has been Bollington's venue for festivals and carnivals, for the celebration of coronations and military victories. Few who stood here by the rushing river to watch the new millennium fireworks against the dark looming background of Swinerood Wood, Clarence Mill and canal embankment will quickly forget the experience.

The Recreation Ground stands where the Dean Valley is at its narrowest, a natural crossing point. A bridge had been built over

the river on Adlington Road by the 17th century. In the late 1820s, the engineers of the Macclesfield Canal constructed the massive embankment and aqueduct. Forty years later came the Macclesfield, Bollington and Marple Railway (now the Middlewood Way). It is said that arches were insisted on, rather than an embankment, to allow westerly breezes to ventilate the valley. Nonetheless, the area was known as the Gnat Hole till recent times.

Francis Greg, a member of the cotton dynasty, provided here a playing field for the Bollington Cricket Club, with pavilion and bandstand, in the 1880s. When Greg died in 1901, the ground was left to the Urban District Council for public use.

Bollington's surprisingly prominent Cricket Club retained effective control of the ground for many years. County cricket was played here before the first world war. The Club's annual Whitsun Sports were regarded as the best in the north, and attracted champion athletes from all over the country. Special trains from Manchester and the Potteries brought thousands of visitors to Bollington and its Recreation Ground.

2. HOUGH HOLE

Hough Hole was the site of a water-powered cotton mill, one of nine built on the River Dean and its tributaries in the township of Rainow between 1784 and 1806. Hough Hole Mill was built in 1803 by local farmer and builder James Mellor, who had previously bought Hough Hole House and farm.

James Mellor's son William, and William's sons, later established an engineering business at the mill. In addition to their renowned precision lathes and steam hammers, William Mellor and Sons produced a three wheeled metal steam carriage, which could carry twenty people at between four and eight miles per hour. On the trial journey from Rainow over the hills to Swythamley, the machine consumed 2.5 cwt of common coke.

William's brother, James Mellor Jnr. (1796-1891), retired early from business, and applied his energy and inventiveness to a wide range of projects. He acted as village dentist, set up his own printing press, installed a water powered organ at Hough Hole House which he could play while lying in bed – the bed itself would convert into a writing desk.

In his youth James Jnr had been the superintendent of Rainow Sunday School; in the second half of his long life he preached general Christian principles to congregations which met in a tabernacle, known as "Bethel", at Hough Hole House. He had discovered the writings of Swedenborg, and loved to expound them while conducting visitors to his "allegorical garden" around a route which corresponded to Pilgrim's Progress.

3. INGERSLEY VALE MILL

Toward the end of 1999, the older part of Ingersley Vale Mill was gutted by fire. Only the walls are standing and these represent a rebuilding after a disastrous fire in 1819. A large stone in the mill frontage bears the date 1809, but in fact the first mill on the site, a cotton mill, was erected in 1792 or 1793.

The wheelhouse, taller than the factory itself, appears by its style to have been built around the middle of the 19th century. Water was brought from a pool upstream along a valley side leat which can still be seen, and across a metal trough above the road, and fed onto the top of a huge waterwheel.

A newspaper reporter paid a visit in 1935: "Climbing up into a dank cold room I saw a waterwheel of amazing size. It is the largest working water wheel in the country – 56 feet in diameter and 10 feet 6 inches across the buckets." By this time the wheel was being used to drive a dynamo to supply electricity to the mill. It is said that the rumble of the wheel was so loud that it could be heard on still days in the centre of Bollington. **LE**

Palmerston Street, Bollington

Congleton

LENGTH OF WALK: Approximately 5 miles
DEGREE OF DIFFICULTY: Easy
PUBLIC TRANSPORT: Congleton is on the Stockport-Stoke on Trent railway line. This walk passes within yards of Congleton station.
ORDNANCE SURVEY MAP: At 1:25000 , this walk can be found on Pathfinder Map 776 (Congleton).

From Congleton's gothic town hall we walk through the centre of the town to the remains of one of Cheshire's earliest silk mills. We walk through the municipal park, and follow the River Dane upstream before joining the Biddulph Valley Way, the former railway from Congleton to Biddulph and the Potteries. The trackbed climbs out of Congleton steeply, passing under the main Manchester-Stoke line. Beyond, the former junction of the two railways is obscured by scrubby trees and undergrowth. We leave the Biddulph Valley way along the towpath of the Macclesfield Canal, passing on a high aqueduct over the Dane in Shaw Brook and then through Hightown. Beyond the Canal Street wharf, we leave the canal to walk down ancient shady Lambert's Lane as far as the dark hollow where it crosses the Howty Brook. A path through Priesty Fields leads us back to the town; we pass the elegant stuccoed houses of Moody Street and the tucked-away church of St Peter's on our way back to the town hall.

This walk begins at Congleton Town Hall (opened 1866). From the town hall, walk along High Street toward the town centre. Continue ahead through the pedestrianised area, then turn right into Mill Street. After a few yards the large (formerly silk) mills at Stonehouse Green can be seen on the right.

Walk down Mill Street to the large traffic island at the head of Mountbatten Way. Bear left, and cross the River Dane by the iron bridge (dated 1889). Turn immediately right, into Mill Green. The remains of Congleton's oldest silk mill, Old Mill (1753) are on the right. At the end of Mill Green, close to the site of the town's Old Corn Mill, a side entrance leads into **Congleton Park (1)**.

Where the park opens out, follow the path on the left, at the bottom of the wooded brow. At the far end of the park, follow the path which runs above the river. The path joins an industrial estate road. On the other side of the river can be seen evidence of mills which were all at some time silk mills.

Where the road swings to the left, cross the Dane by the footbridge on the right. Turn right into Havannah Street. Take the first street on the left, King Street, which leads to the A54, the former Congleton-Buxton turnpike. Cross the main road, and follow the track (Tommy's Lane) which is almost opposite.

Walk past the first house on the right, and the field beyond. Before the next house, turn right and follow the footway down to the brook. A former silk mill site is on the left, behind the wall. Cross the footbridge, climb the steps under the bridge, then turn right for access to the former Biddulph branch of the **North Staffordshire Railway (2)**, now the Biddulph Valley Way. Turn right onto the trackbed, and cross over the bridge you have just walked under.

Our route now follows the former railway for almost a mile. The Biddulph branch climbed up to pass under the North Staffordshire Railway main line, now part of the line from London to Manchester via Stoke. Just beyond, the embankment of the spur which formed a connection with the main line descends gently to join the Biddulph branch line.

Continue along the former railway as far as a gate, beyond which the Macclesfield Canal (opened 1831) crosses the line. Take the steps on the right here, which lead up to the canal. Turn right onto the towpath. The canal crosses the steep valley of the Dane in Shaw Brook, providing a good view of the railway viaduct downstream.

Half a mile further on, at the Congleton suburb of Hightown, the canal passes under three bridges in quick succession. The old stone bridge, numbered bridge 75, carried the road from Biddulph, which crossed the railway by a level crossing just outside Congleton station (which is on the right). This was replaced by the flyover, crossing both railway and canal, when the railway was electrified. To the left, between the road and railway bridges, is the site of the feedstuffs milling factory.

Continue along the canal towpath. Bridge 76 is a snake or

turnover bridge, allowing the towpath to change sides. An iron aqueduct carries the canal over Canal Street; beyond is the site of Congleton wharf, with its elegant but derelict nineteenth century warehouse. Congleton's canal wharf and main railway station were both a good three-quarters of a mile from the town centre.

We leave the canal towpath at the next bridge (77), which is also a turnover bridge. Cross the bridge on the towpath, then climb the steps on the right which lead up to Lambert's Lane, a very old trackway from the west, which was possibly part of a prehistoric route up to the Bridestones, and was used in later days as a saltway and as a drovers' road. Turn left, and follow the track. After about a third of a mile, the surfaced track swings sharply to the left, but we continue straight ahead through a gate on the original lane, now a green way.

The lane descends into the valley of a brook known as the Howty. Where it takes on the character of a dark sunken holloway, before a foot bridge over the brook, take the field path on the right. After a few yards it is necessary to wade or jump over a very small stream. The path in the field beyond is faintly visible: keep well up on the valley side, to pass above a sandy landslip.

The path then descends, and a stile leads into a narrow, rather muddy, hedged track which has the look of a packhorse trail. A path which joins from the left has crossed the Howty on a surprisingly grand stone bridge with railings.

The path leads to a road, Priesty Fields. The name may be derived from the route taken by the priests of Congleton to the mother church at Astbury. Vale Mill (silk, then fustian cutting) can be seen, built across the valley. Priesty Fields road swings to the right, and leads to the foot of Howey Lane. Here, turn left into Moody Street, then right into Chapel Street. **St. Peter's Church (3)** lies ahead.

Walk past the church, down to Albert Place. Turn left to return to our starting point, the town hall.

1. CONGLETON PARK

Congleton's municipal park, opened in 1871, came rather late - Macclesfield's West Park had opened 17 years earlier.

Congleton Corporation had possessed for centuries what many of the townsfolk had come to regard as the natural nucleus of a park: the Town's Wood, on the northern bank of the Dane. In 1865, the corporation acquired the land between the wood and the river. Access problems on the town side of the river were eventually solved, and funds raised by subscription for a new road across 'the Meadows' and an iron bridge over the river, which was designed and constructed by Mr Edwin Scragg, "the well known mechanical engineer of Buglawton".

The park was laid out by the borough treasurer, and Mr Kemp of Birkenhead. Paths ran up through the wood to the Crimean War trophy cannon, installed at the top. Below the

Congleton's Crimean Cannon, melted down during World War 2.

29

wood was a quarter mile terraced walk, with drinking fountains. By the river, a bowling green. In between was a recreation ground "where cricket and other manly sports can be engaged in."

The formal opening took place on Whit Monday, 29th May 1871. A procession of councillors, dignitaries, and friendly societies arrived at the park. Dr Beales, in place of the mayor (who was recuperating from illness at Buxton), performed the ceremony. "Let no immoral or impure act defile this sacred spot" warned the doctor. The Russian cannon fired several discharges in rapid succession.

The councillors and dignitaries retired to lunch in the mayor's parlour. Meanwhile (in the words of the newspaper) "thousands of the population assembled in the park... some to rusticate in the wood, others to bivouac on the banks of the river, while some were witnessing the sports, and not a few enjoying the new privilege of airing their wives and sweethearts in the boats just placed on the river by the parks committee."

2. THE NORTH STAFFORDSHIRE RAILWAY

The North Staffordshire Railway Company's line from Macclesfield to Stoke and beyond was fully opened in 1849. The line skirts Congleton to the east, crossing the Dane in Shaw Brook, a tributary of the Dane, on a ten arch brick viaduct, 697 feet long with a maximum height above the stream of 107 feet.

Ten years later the NSR opened a branch line from Brunswick Road Wharf, Congleton, via Biddulph, to the Potteries, mainly to serve the coal mines of the Biddulph valley. The northern part of this line was closed in 1969, and the trackbed now forms the Biddulph Valley Way.

The Biddulph branch line passed under the main line just north of the Dane in Shaw viaduct. A connection was provided here by a short spur from Upper Junction on the main line to Lower Junction on the branch line.

From the Lower Junction the branch line drops steeply down to the goods wharf at Brunswick Street. It was here that a coal train consisting of a large tank engine, fourteen waggons, and a brake van careered out of control on Christmas Eve, 1895. A gale had blown sand off the slippery rails, according to the newspaper account, so that the brakes failed to act. As the train ran down the incline "at a great rate" the driver blew the whistle before he and the stoker jumped clear. This alerted the fourteen men who were unloading coal from eight trucks into horse drawn carts in the sidings below, and no lives were lost as the runaway train smashed into and demolished the trucks. A breakdown gang from Stoke had to work through Christmas Day and Boxing Day to clear the wreckage before the line could be repaired.

3. ST. PETER'S CHURCH

Until 1868, St. Peter's Church, albeit the town's 'civic' church, was technically a chapel of the mother church in the nearby village of Astbury. Congleton, long the more important place, had two chapels by the later Middle Ages. One chapel stood by the bridge over the Dane at the foot of Rood Hill. Out of use by the early 17th century, this served for some time as a bell foundry and later as a workhouse. No trace remains today. St. Peter's stands on the site of the medieval "upper chapel". The latest rebuilding was in 1752 (though the upper part of the tower was not erected until 1786).

It seems likely that the upper chapel was originally dedicated not just to St. Peter, but to St. Peter ad Vincula (St. Peter in Chains). The timing of Congleton wakes in August corresponds to the feast of that name in the Roman Catholic calendar.

The Wakes holiday was preceded by a vigil (hence "wake"). In Congleton, it seems, the waking for the vigil was encouraged by the procession around the town of servers wearing large bells on leather sashes, representing the chains of St. Peter's imprisonment.

At the Reformation, the chains were secularised, and were ultimately acquired by a dynasty of chimney sweeps, the Stubbs family, who "zealously guarded what they termed their hereditary right, perpetuating among hideous rows and drunken fracas the annual perambulation of the borough" (Robert Head, Byegone Cheshire, 1895).

In the 19th century, John Wilson, town clerk and 'King of Congleton', put an end to the uproar by taking advantage of a disputed succession among the Stubbses, buying out both sides, and putting the chains safely in the Town Council archives. **LE**

St Peter's Church, Congleton

Gradbach – Lud's Church – Danebridge

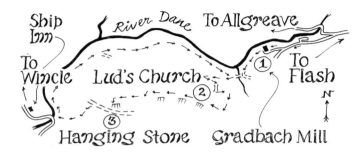

LENGTH OF WALK: Approximately seven miles.
DEGREE OF DIFFICULTY: Moderate.
ORDNANCE SURVEY MAP: At 1:25000, this walk can be found on
Outdoor Leisure Map 24 (The Peak District – White Peak Area).

*This walk begins where the youthful River Dane flows down from
high moorland, dividing Cheshire from Staffordshire. We walk past
isolated Gradbach Mill, now a Youth Hostel, following the Dane to a
tributary stream, the Black Brook, at the point below Back Forest
where an ancient rural iron foundry once stood. We climb up
through pine and birch to the mysterious rocky cleft known as Lud's
Church, then walk on through open moor to the crest of a ridge
which provides sweeping views across the hills and valleys of the
Staffordshire Moorlands. We drop down past the Hanging Stone, a
place of sinister legend, to the wooded valley at Danebridge, before
following the Dane upstream to our starting point.*

This walk begins at the car park beside the River Dane at
Gradbach (map ref. 998 663). To find this rather remote site on the
Cheshire/Staffordshire border turn off the A 54 Congleton-Buxton
road at the Rose and Crown, Allgreave, and follow the minor road
for about two miles. After the bridge over the Dane, turn very
sharply right onto the track which leads toward the Youth Hostel at
Gradbach Mill. The car park, which is a few hundred yards down
the track, takes only thirty or so cars, and fills rapidly on fine
summer weekends, so an early start is advisable.

From the car park, turn right and walk along the quiet lane.
After a few hundred yards, massive stone gateposts and a YHA sign
show the way to **Gradbach Mill (1).**

Walk round to the front of the mill, then follow the path on the left, which leads to steps and a stile. Follow the well worn path down the valley to the point where, having become a stone track, it twists round to the left. Here, go through the gap in the stone wall on the right, climb down the steps, and walk down to the footbridge over the Black Brook, which is known as Casters Bridge. (You may have noticed pieces of iron slag in the path, apparently taken from the slag heap of a long-vanished local foundry.)

Across the bridge follow the path through the trees straight up the hillside, past two sets of fingerposts, before taking the highest path to the right. This path rises gently through woods of birch and pine for about a quarter of a mile. Opposite an outcrop of dissected rocks (Castle Cliffs), take the path to the left, signed to Lud's Church.

The narrow entrance to the rocky ravine of **Lud's Church (2)** is a few hundred yards along the path, on the right. Cool air spilling from the cleft marks the spot on a hot day. Walk down into and through the natural chasm. At the far end, steps lead up to the surface, where the path leads to the left. Follow this path as it gently descends to meet another path. Here turn right - the path is marked "Concession path to the ridge" and is not shown on the OS map.

The concession path climbs quite steeply up through heather moorland to a notch in the ridge. From the top, Tittesworth Reservoir can be seen in the distance to the left; Gun Hill lies ahead across the valley; and far away to the right can be seen the profile of Bosley Cloud.

a short detour from the walk will bring you to Danebridge

Follow the well used ridge top path (another concession path) to the right. Where the path descends and joins another path from the right, turn left, pass the gate, and walk into the nick in the hill. Take the concession path on the right which leads over the wall and across fields to the **Hanging Stone (3)**. The stone is approached from above. Steps on the right lead down to the base and the memorial plaque.

Walk down to the farm track below, and turn right. Behind Hangingstone Farm, take the field path on the left, signed to Danebridge. Beyond a wall, the path leads straight down a field past a standing stone to a narrow valley in the larch woods ahead. Follow the path above the main stream, and walk straight down through the woods to the River Dane.

To return direct to Gradbach, turn right on the path beside the Dane. But if you have by now worked up a thirst you might want to turn left, cross the bridge over the Dane, and walk for a few hundred yards up the road to the Ship Inn.

Return to the bridge, then turn left on to the path by the river. This path rises and falls through fields and woods, following the hillside above the Dane to return to Casters Bridge. The path is easily followed, and waymarked in places.

Two buildings are passed. Beyond the first, Back Dane, carry straight on where the track goes round to the right. Walk straight past the second – the path here is waymarked. Beyond, we re-enter the Roaches Estate. The Dane Valley becomes rocky and narrow, and the path is never far from the tumbling stream. After about three quarters of a mile, at a junction of paths, walk down to Casters Bridge, and return to the starting point via Gradbach Mill.

1. GRADBACH MILL

Until recently, the early history of Gradbach Mill has been written only from local tradition. Display boards at the mill reflect the old story that the mill was built in 1640, and rebuilt in or around 1780. But the recently published Leek and Moorlands volume of the Victoria County History of Staffordshire has a properly documented account of the origin of the mill.

The site was leased from Sir Henry Harpur in 1792 by Thomas and James Oliver of Longnor and Thomas White of Hartington, to build a water powered cotton mill. The mill was converted to flax spinning by the Dakeyne family of Darley in 1798, and Dakeynes continued to operate the mill until 1868, latterly for silk waste spinning.

The style of the mill indicates that a re-building took place, probably in the 1830s or 1840s, which is rather late for investment in such a remote site. Local tradition of a disastrous fire at the mill is strong; the mill may have been rebuilt with the insurance money.

It has been claimed that 200 people worked at the mill in its heyday, though the maximum figure was probably more like the 64 recorded for 1838. Some would walk to work daily along field paths and moorland tracks from nearby settlements such as Flash, England's highest village. Others lived in cottage terraces near the

mill, of which only the faintest traces now survive.

After its closure for silk spinning, the mill was put to use as a sawmill for the Harpur Crewe Estate. Later, when the adjacent mill manager's house became a farm house, the mill was used as a barn, and the structure began to deteriorate. Salvation came in 1978, when the Youth Hostels Association bought the land and buildings. The mill and manager's house were converted into a hostel, which opened in 1984.

2. LUD'S CHURCH

Why is this natural ravine called a church? In the depths, a cool cathedral calm prevails. But has Lud's Church actually been used for worship?

Doug Pickford appears to be convinced that this place was sacred to "the Celtic sky god Lud" – and that the Dane was named after "the earth-mother Dana." (Myths and Legends of East Cheshire and the Moorlands, 1992) Others have thought Lud to be a corruption of Hood, and that Robin Hood came here to pray. Another much-repeated tradition has Lollards, early persecuted protestants, meeting in Lud's Church for secret services.

It has been argued strongly that Lud's Church can be identified with the Green Chapel, the scene of the denouement of the

down what becomes a flagged path leading to Clough Mill, a former cotton mill which is said to have been started in 1796, but which has been rebuilt and extended many times. Cotton production here ceased in 1928. The mill buildings were put to various uses before conversion to flats in the early 1990s.

Footbridges cross the two streams which meet here. The path leads to the front of the former mill. Turn right at the road, and follow it to a bridge over the river, and up the steep bank beyond. Primrose Vale Mill was sited in the valley below. Tanning, paper making, fustian cutting, and colour pigment manufacture all seem to have taken place on this site.

Where the road turns sharply right, carry straight on along the footpath. The pool of Bankvale Mill can be seen through the trees in the valley below. Where the path splits, take the lower route, closer to the river bank, which descends to a group of cottages, crossing a dry mill leat. Walk along the quiet tarmac road ahead. Bankvale Mill, which is said to have been established in 1791, and operated until quite recently as a paper mill, can be seen on the right through the trees.

At the road junction beyond Oaklands, a large nineteenth century house, turn left into Swallowhouse Road (not sharp left into Swallowhouse Avenue). After a few hundred yards, shortly before the by-pass flyover, go through a wooden gate on the right, and follow the path down by the river and under the by-pass into the village of **Hayfield (3)**.

The track beyond the by-pass is called Mill Street – Hayfield's corn mill stood here until the mid nineteenth century. Turn right on Market Street. After one block, the memorial garden on the right provides a good view of the former Grotto Mill. Continue along the road and cross the bridge, after which turn right onto the path between the church and the river. Follow the churchyard wall round to the left. Where the tarmac begins, carry straight on, keeping the restaurant to your left, to find the underpass which leads back to the starting point on the other side of the by-pass.

1. THE SETT VALLEY TRAIL

The Sett Valley Trail runs along the trackbed of the former railway from New Mills to Hayfield, which was built by the Manchester, Sheffield and Lincolnshire Railway Company. The three mile line, single track almost all the way, opened on March 1st, 1868 – a day of brilliant sunshine which followed overnight snow. Hayfield turned out en masse to greet the first train up the track, on which the New Mills Band had travelled, playing throughout the journey.

The line served the calico printing works which had been established in the Sett Valley in the first half of the nineteenth century, and it helped the expansion of many of them in the later part of the century. The line brought fuel and provisions and passenger services to Birch Vale and Hayfield, where the only stations were sited.

Visitors outnumbered local passengers on summer weekends, as Hayfield became the gateway to the high moorlands for

Manchester ramblers. By the 1930s up to 5,000 people might arrive by train on a summer Sunday. Benny Rothman has described the scene on Manchester's London Road Station as the ramblers began their journey to Hayfield: "the platform rang to the sound of nailed boots." Kinder Scout itself remained closed to ramblers, for the sake of the grouse. Rothman was one of those imprisoned after the Kinder Trespass of 1932, which began with a mass meeting on a recreation ground in Hayfield.

While the visitors were no doubt welcome commercially, the scale of the weekend invasions caused some friction. Crichton Porteous wrote that "the playing of ukeleles, accordions, melodions and other instruments on Sunday evenings was once so bad that the people of Hayfield were driven to making public protests" (*Peakland*, 1954).

The closure of the railway in 1970 was a great blow to the communities involved, as was usually the case with Beeching's victims. In this case the damage was partly offset by Derbyshire County Council's purchase of the line in 1973, and the opening of the Sett Valley Trail in 1979.

2. THE LOST MILLS OF ROWARTH

The remains of Rowarth's lost mills are few and hard to detect, but a visit to Rowarth nonetheless provides a good idea of what the small industrial communities of the early industrial revolution must have looked like: overwhelmingly rural still, with small mills along the streams and isolated terraces and chapels scattered about in the fields.

Water powered mills for carding and spinning cotton sprang up widely in the western Pennine foothills from the mid 1780s, when Richard Arkwright's patents were no longer an obstacle. Small streams were sufficient to power the early mills, provided there was a good fall of water on the site.

Five cotton mills were built along the brook at Rowarth, and another at nearby Ringstones, in the late eighteenth and early nineteenth centuries. Such enterprises typically leave few or no written records, so exact dates of opening cannot usually be given. Small though the mills were, local labour was apparently insufficient: all nine houses in Poplar Row (built 1812) were occupied by cotton spinners most of whom had been born outside Derbyshire, according to the census of 1841.

Social provision for the people of industrial Rowarth included five pubs and a Chapel/Sunday School, but little else. For Rowarth's industrial development was choked off soon after it had begun, by the absence of good roads and the inadequacy of the stream to sustain expansion. Eileen Miller, in her booklet *The Lost Mills of Rowarth* (New Mills History Notes No 8, 1984) says that bankruptcies among the mill owners began as early as 1806, and she notes that the Stockport Advertiser, between 1822 (when it began) and 1835 carried eleven notices of auction of Rowarth mills, and six bankruptcies.

By the twentieth century all the mills had been abandoned. All that remains is a few overgrown mounds, stretches of ruined stone

wall here and there, suggestions of water channels, and boggy and clogged mill pool sites.

3. HAYFIELD

Hayfield has been a route centre for centuries – in fact, the Roman road from Melandra Castle near Glossop to Buxton passed this way. By the early modern period, carts and waggons could travel north from Hayfield to Glossop and via Longdendale over to Yorkshire; south via Chapel en le Frith and Buxton; west to Marple, Stockport and Manchester; and packhorse trains could travel eastwards around Kinder Scout into the Ashop Valley or into Edale.

Hayfield's position on major routes probably encouraged specialisation in the woollen industry – Manchester and Stockport merchants would "put out" spinning and weaving to be carried on domestically. Weavers' garretts can still be seen in the village. Walk Mill Road indicates that Hayfield also had a walk mill, or water powered fulling mill for woollen cloth.

Grotto Mill in the village centre is usually said to have been built in the late 1780s as a woollen mill, but it seems likely that this was the mill advertised in the Manchester Mercury in 1787 and again in 1790 as "a new erected cotton mill ... now used for carding cotton wool ... in the centre of the improving town of Hayfield."

In the nineteenth century, bleaching, printing and papermaking began just downstream, and steam power was adopted. Louis J Jennings wrote that there was "always plenty of smoke" at Hayfield. He added that "at night there are no lights in the streets after March, but that is not of much consequence, for there is nothing whatever to see" (*Rambles Among the Hills*, 1880).

A normally quiet place perhaps, but storms over the moors could cause high drama as torrents of water poured through the village. John Wesley described such a flood in 1748 in his Journal: "rocks were loosened from the mountains, one field was covered from side to side with massive boulders, some water mills were washed away without any remains, trees were torn up by the roots and whirled away like stubble, two women of loose character were swept away from their own door and drowned ..." Floods swamped the church and washed bodies and bones out of the churchyard, and several times swept away the nearby bridge. The church was therefore rebuilt in 1818, with a raised floor level; the bridge was likewise raised in 1837, which is why the bottom storeys of houses to the north of the bridge are below the present level of the street. LE

the weir at Hayfield

the bridge at Hayfield

Hope to Castleton

Edale

Back Tor

Hollins Cross

③

Hope Valley Line
to New Mills
and Manchester

N

① Peak Cavern
② Mam Tor
③ Ward's Piece

Hope

Hope Station

② A 625 (B6049)
to Tideswell

Castleton

The Winnats

①

Quarries

LENGTH OF WALK: approximately eight miles.

DEGREE OF DIFFICULTY: medium.

PUBLIC TRANSPORT: the starting point of this walk, Hope Station, is on the Hope Valley railway line between Manchester and Sheffield. Trains which stop at Hope can be caught from Marple, New Mills Central and Chinley. Most of the bus services through Hope to Castleton come from the eastern or southern sides of the Peak District, though there is an infrequent service from Buxton.

ORDNANCE SURVEY MAP: At 1:25,000, this walk can be found on Outdoor Leisure Map No 1: The Peak District, Dark Peak Area.

From the old religious centre and market village of Hope, where the medieval salters from Cheshire rested their pack horse trains overnight on cross-Peak journeys, we follow on this walk a well-worn path through fields by the Peakshole Water to Castleton, a medieval settlement on a gridiron pattern built below the Norman Peveril Castle. Through narrow back streets we walk to Goosehill bridge, which crosses the Peakshole Water close to its source, the great gloomy Peak Cavern. Field paths climb gently past the entrance to the dramatic Winnats Pass, past the Speedwell and Treak Cliff Caverns, toward the workings of the old Odin lead mine. We walk over the buckled and shattered remains of the former main road, unwisely built across the foot of the Mam Tor landslip, before climbing rather less gently than before to the top of the high ridge which provides sweeping views across Edale to the Kinder plateau and the high bleak moorland to the north. The ridge top is followed to the summit of Lose Hill, to the viewfinder on Ward's Piece, before the easy descent through green fields back to Hope.

This walk begins at Hope railway station. If you arrive by car rather than by train, you may choose to start the walk at Hope village which is about half a mile up the road – though on busy days you may find it easier to park near the station. If you do drive to Hope, it is best to avoid driving through Castleton, one of the busiest "honeypots" of the Peak District, on summer weekends and bank holidays. This can be done by approaching through Tideswell, or from Sparrowpit on the A623 across Tideswell Moor, then taking the B6049 through Bradwell to Brough, then turning left on the A625 toward Hope and Castleton.

From the approach road to Hope Station, turn right and follow the footpath beside the A625 into Hope village. Turn left beyond the parish church of St. Peter, into Pindale Road. Just over Watergates bridge, you will see Hope pinfold on the right. Follow the road up the hill for a few hundred yards, then take the signed path on the right which leads through the fields to Castleton. This is a very well used path, so detailed directions should not be necessary. We cross the branch railway line which leads to the notorious cement works, established in this inappropriate spot in 1928. Further on, mounds in the fields mark the line of a sough or drainage tunnel from lead mines in the hills to the left. Peveril Castle and the Mam Tor landslip scar can be seen on the skyline ahead. Where the path becomes a trackway, the ruined shell of an early cotton spinning mill can be seen on the right.

The track joins the main road into Castleton. Turn left, and walk for a few yards to Mill Lane, which is on the right. Follow this track round between former corn mill buildings. At the road beyond, turn left. The stream by the road is the leat carrying water to the old mill.

Walk up to the junction with the main road, and continue straight on. Where the main road swings right, carry straight on along Back Street to the village green. Here bear right, and take the narrow lane to the left of the YHA building, which leads past

the chip shop down towards **Peak Cavern (1)**. At the bottom of the hill, just across Goosehill Bridge, is the path (on the left) which leads to Peak Cavern. It is worth walking up to look at the entrance, even if you don't want the guided tour of the interior on this occasion.

Return to Goosehill Bridge. Our route climbs Goosehill. As you climb, keep to the right, on what becomes a narrow track. Past the walls of the grounds of Goosehill Hall, go through the higher of two gates. A field path, gently rising, follows the highest wall of the Castleton fields to join the Winnats road just below the Speedwell Cavern, where visitors travel underground by boat along a lead mine sough constructed in the 1770s.

Turn left and go over the stile which is a little higher up the road, on the right. Cross the field to pass above the small wood ahead. Further on, the path joins the steep approach to the Treak Cliff Cavern, where "Blue John" has been mined since the eighteenth century. Walk down the path to the road, and turn left. After a few hundred yards, the iron ore-crushing circle of the Odin lead mine can be seen on the right. Whether the name indicates a Saxon or Danish origin is debatable, but the mine is probably a very old one, as the lead outcropped here – where there is now a narrow cleft, to the left of the road.

Beyond the Odin Mine, the road has been closed to all but farm traffic. **Mam Tor (2)**, with its huge landslip scar, looms above. Walk along the twisted and cracked roadway to the point where the road swung sharply round to the left. Take the path on the right which passes above Mam Farm and the fenced off woodland. This path can be followed easily around the hillside and then diagonally up to the slight notch in the ridge known as Hollins Cross, where seven packhorse trails converged.

Edale lies below. Though the valley was remote and inaccessible before the railway was opened in 1894, a cotton spinning mill had been built here by 1793. The mill, later extended and now converted into flats, can be seen directly below. Turn right at Hollins Cross and follow the path along the top of the ridge. After half a mile, where the path splits, cross the stile to the left and continue ahead directly up the steep slope of Back Tor. Continue along the top of the ridge to the summit of Lose Hill, which now bears on Ordnance Survey maps the alternative name of **Ward's Piece (3)**.

From the viewfinder, continue along the flagged path which begins the descent toward Hope, which can be seen below. At the bottom of the initial steep slope, cross the stile and continue straight on to a second stile. Cross, and follow the fence down the hill. The path is easy to follow. It swings right then left towards a farm. Bear left above the farm, go through the blue gate, then turn right, cross a stile, and walk down the field with the wall to your right. At the end of the wall, bear left across the field and cross a stile by a barn. Continue downhill. The path is not clear, but the way can be found by following the stiles and yellow marker posts. Towards the bottom of the hill the path follows for a while a small green lane, overhung by branches. Continue straight past a house and cross the cement works branch line by a dipping footbridge. Stiles indicate the route across the fields beyond.

Goosehill

Just past an old caravan parked by the path, turn left and walk across to a stile, and down to the Hope-Edale road. If you turn right here you can follow the road into Hope village. If you have started the walk at Hope Station, you may prefer to return part of the way alongside the River Noe. If so, cross the road and turn left down the smaller lane which leads to Killhill Bridge. Take the track on the right beyond the bridge, which follows the mill leat (on the left) to the former Hope corn mill. Walk round the building. A footpath (on the left, signed, but not easy to spot) continues at a higher level along the riverbank to emerge at Netherhall Bridge below Hope. Turn left at the road to return to the railway station.

1. PEAK CAVERN

Peak Cavern lies below Peveril Castle at the foot of a cleft in the limestone hill which was known even in polite society as "the Arse of the Peak" from the time of the Domesday Book (which locates the castle 'in peches ers') down to the late eighteenth century. Indeed, the wealthy folk who visited this "wonder of the Peak" would often be told that they were entering "the Devil's Arse". The infernal regions, it was suggested, lay not far beyond the half mile or so of accessible caverns. Had not the old woman's goose which fell down Eldon Hole on the hills above emerged three days later from the Peak Cavern with singed feathers?

The connection between the swallow holes of Rushup Vale and the Peak Cavern is quite real. Streams which flow down from the gritstone edge sink through the limestone in joints and fissures, some of which have been dissolved and eroded into cave systems, to emerge below in Castleton. Many of the caverns of the area have been enlarged by miners seeking lead or "Blue John". This seems not to have happened to any great extent in the Peak Cavern, though the very large cave entrance was put to economic use from the 18th century as an all-weather rope walk. In the 19th century, romantic visitors to the cavern sought a solemn, profound experience, and objected to the noise and clamour of the rope makers. To compensate, the parish choir could be hired out to sing ethereally, perched on elevated parts of the illuminated rocks.

By the beginning of the 20th century the village "overflows with the tripper ... and its streets are apt to be uproarious until the last brakes have gone singing down the vale" (J B Firth: *Highways and Byways in Derbyshire*, 1905). Rope making in the Peak Cavern survived into these less fastidious times, and continued on a regular basis until the 1970s.

2. MAM TOR

Mam Tor is a name which may have come down to us from the Celtic Iron Age, meaning "mother hill" or perhaps "breast shaped hill". Mam Tor was clearly a place of great prehistoric significance. Even today, the remains of a massive ditch and rampart which enclosed around 16 acres of the hilltop can be seen clearly. Within, over a hundred hut-platforms have been detected. Until quite recently, this was assumed to be a large hill fort of the Iron Age

(circa 800BC-70AD), but radio carbon dating of charcoal found at a hut site has given a Bronze Age date of around 1200 BC. The site also contains two barrows which may be older still.

Whatever the nature of the settlement here, it seems likely that the site was chosen at least partly to control a major east-west route through the Peak. The same consideration led the Romans to build a fort at Brough, a mile or so below Hope, and the Normans to build the castle at Castleton.

Early travellers to the west may have left the Hope Valley through the Winnats (or "wind gate", meaning "windy way"). This was the route taken by the turnpike road established under an Act of 1758. Steep stretches of early turnpikes were often by-passed later as traffic increased: hence the new road (abandoned since

1977) built across the Mam Tor landslip under an Act of 1811.

The new road was fairly steep too, and passengers on the Sheffield-Manchester coaches still had to get out and walk up the worst parts. Here they might encounter the ubiquitous "Daft Sammy", self-styled Castleton Guide. A dialect account, published five years after Sammy's death in Chapel-en-le-Frith workhouse in 1865, described his exploits. When the passengers disembarked at the foot of Mam Tor, "Sammy 'ud gravely stretch aat 'is 'ond [hand] an' ax wun o' th' passingers ta ta'e owd [take hold] on 't an' for t' next ta ley owd i' same wey till they war aw [all] i' a loine [line], wen Sammy ud pull wi' aw 'is strength ta get 'em up th' 'ill." (Reprinted in the *Sheffield Clarion Ramblers Handbook*, 1940-41.)

3. WARD'S PIECE
The summit of Lose Hill, acquired by the National Trust in 1945, is dedicated to the memory of George Herbert Bridges Ward (1876-1957). GHB Ward (Bert to his friends), as a young man with unruly thick black hair and dark piercing eyes, strode across the moors at the head of the Sheffield Clarion Ramblers, defiantly walking ancient closed footpaths and facing down the landowners and their gamekeepers.

Ward started his working life as a fitter and toolmaker in Sheffield, and became a local government officer and labour adviser, and served as the first Secretary of the Sheffield Labour Representation Committee. He saw rambling as the opportunity for the working men and women of the industrial towns to re-establish a sense of fellowship, and oneness with nature. After being sacked as a Sunday School teacher for advocating Sunday rambling, Ward founded the Sheffield Clarion Ramblers in 1900. The club became one of the leading northern rambling clubs, and Ward organised it as its secretary right up to his death, while also playing an important national role in the struggle for access to mountains.

Ward provided "hints" for the leaders of rambles: "the ramble will be taken, wet or fine ... the leader will wear a distinctive badge, and appoint a whipper-in ... he is expected to provide a reading, or to give useful information upon the way from the Ramblers' booklet or other sources, and to see that some song is sung during the day ..."

Ward's best memorial is the long run of the annual Sheffield Clarion Ramblers Handbook, for here Ward published the fruits of his tireless researches, using documents and maps to trace the ancient packhorse trails and ways, and oral sources to record the lore of the Peak. "The restorer of paths became in time the intimate chronicler of obscure men – the mason at the roadside wall, the shepherd on the hills, the farm hand son of a farm hand. These men turned over their store of memories to him; from them he learned not only how and where they lived, but the ways their forefathers trod. Bit by bit, here a little and there a little, he gleaned the facts of long usage, of old tracks lost, disused, or filched; of fields and farms and enclosures; right and wrong of all sorts. From alehouse and tavern he gleaned, and spoke to all and sundry on the road ..." (Joseph W Batty, in *SCR Handbook*, 1949-50). LE

Knutsford and Tatton Park

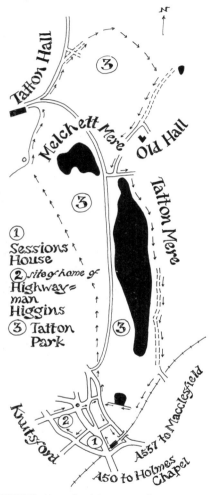

LENGTH OF WALK: Approximately seven miles.

DEGREE OF DIFFICULTY: Low

PUBLIC TRANSPORT: Knutsford Station is on the railway line from Manchester, Stockport and Altrincham to Northwich and Chester. Bus services from Macclesfield, Wilmslow, Altrincham and Northwich call at Knutsford.

ORDNANCE SURVEY MAP: At 1:25,000, the northern part of this walk can be found on Pathfinder map 740 (Warrington), and the southern part on Pathfinder map 758 (Northwich and Knutsford).

This walk is partly urban, exploring the genteel old market town of Knutsford, and partly rural, though the countryside involved lies almost entirely within Tatton Park and, while varied and interesting, is a completely artificial creation of the 18th and 19th centuries. We begin at Knutsford railway station, pass the Sessions House, a seat of county administration and justice in the 19th and 20th centuries, and walk round the corner to the site of the home of Highwayman Higgins, who seems to have been taken to Knutsford's heart as a local hero – perhaps as a consequence of the heavy presence of the gentry and magistracy in and around the town. Next door on what is now Gaskell Avenue lived the young Elizabeth Stevenson, who later, as Mrs Gaskell, portrayed Knutsford as the fictional "Cranford". At the head of King Street, almost in the heart of the town, we enter Tatton Park. Entry to the park is free for pedestrians, but note that the gates are not opened until 10 am, and that they are locked at 7pm (earlier in winter). We approach Tatton Hall and its surrounding gardens by a footpath under an avenue of beech trees a mile long, planted in the eighteenth century. We skirt the gardens and Hall (if you wish to go in, an entrance fee has to be paid) and walk across open rolling parkland to the Old Hall, once surrounded by the farms and houses of the village of Tatton, but now isolated. The sunken track of the abandoned old road from Knutsford to Rostherne can been seen nearby, and information boards tell a fascinating history of farming and settlement on the site which goes back to neolithic times. We return to Knutsford along the eastern side of Tatton Mere, where mesolithic people established hunting camps as early as 8000BC. A woodland walk leads back to Knutsford Moor. A path beside the Moor Pool returns us to King Street in the centre of the town.

This walk begins at Knutsford railway station (which was opened in 1862, providing a commuting link for the Manchester merchants who moved into new villas in Knutsford and neighbourhood). If you arrive by train, walk up the steps by the bridge at the end of the platform, and then turn right along Toft Road. On the other side of the road, the former prison governor's house now contains the Council Offices and Information Centre. Cross Toft Road at the pedestrian crossing a little further on. You are now in front of the imposing windowless facade of the **Sessions House (1)**, behind which Knutsford Prison used to stand.

Continue along Toft Road. On the opposite side is the mid-eighteenth century parish church which, happily, has survived the vicissitudes of taste. (Alfred Rimmer, in his *Summer Rambles Around Manchester*, thought that the church was "in the worst style of so-called Hanoverian architecture, and gives everyone a chill as soon as he sees it.") Next to the church is the gothic former Town Market Hall (1870-2), designed by Alfred Waterhouse, paid for by Lord Egerton of Tatton Hall, and now serving as a furniture shop and post office.

Our route lies sharp left beyond the police station, along

Bexton Road. Walk as far as Stanley Road, where the red brick building of the former Bucklow Rural District Council can be seen opposite. Behind it was sited the Altrincham Union Workhouse. Turn right in front of the Bucklow building, and walk between the rows of nineteenth century cottages before turning into Gaskell Avenue, on the right. Knutsford Heath, where the fashionable Knutsford Races were held in the eighteenth century, lies on the left. On the right, Heath House is on the site of the house probably occupied by **Highwayman Higgins (2)**. Next door, Heathwaite House, was the home from 1812 to 1821 of the girl who became Mrs Gaskell.

Walk to the top of Gaskell Avenue, cross King Edward Road by the zebra crossing, and walk past the White Bear into Canute Place. At the end, turn left, then right opposite the Lord Eldon into Minshull Street. At the bottom, turn left into King Street. The entrance to Tatton Park lies ahead. Just in front of it, look to the right: some yards down the street you will see the Ruskin Rooms, one of the vaguely Mediterranean buildings of the Manchester manufacturer Richard Harding Watt which provoked Pevsner to refer to his "remorseless imposing of crazy grandeur on poor Knutsford".

Walk up the path and road which lead to the Knutsford entrance to **Tatton Park (3)**.

Housing was swept away from this area to enhance the dignity of the pedimented arched gateway of 1810, designed by Lewis Wyatt. Inside the park, a path can be found to the left of the driveway beneath an avenue of beeches. A golf course lies just over to the left of the avenue. The avenue continues up to the gardens adjacent to Tatton Hall, and marks the line of an early eighteenth century entrance, abandoned at the suggestion of Humphry Repton (1791) in favour of the present curving driveway which was designed to give a sequence of views of the lake, parkland and Hall.

Walk the whole length of the avenue, continuing beneath the trees when the alignment shifts slightly to the left after about a third of a mile. Tatton Mere can be seen to the right. Nearer to the hall is Melchett Mere, which formed in a hole which appeared in 1922. The Egertons blamed the salt extraction activities of Lord Melchett, of Brunner Mond, Northwich.

At the end of the avenue, beyond a ha-ha, the gardens begin at a folly in the form of a classical rotunda built around 1820. We follow the path to the right which follows the garden boundary for about half a mile. Through the shrubberies we get glimpses of the neo-classical frontage of Tatton Hall, built between 1790 and 1812 to the designs of Samuel and Lewis Wyatt.

Where the garden boundary swings sharply to the left, before the entrance to the grounds of the hall, a junction of tarred driveways can be seen ahead. The farther drive, which runs between a double avenue of trees, is signed *Rostherne exit.* Follow this drive for about a quarter of a mile. It is easy to appreciate here the situation of Tatton, on a ridge of glacial sands and gravels raised above the surrounding boulder clay plain. Take the track which branches off to the right, and continue straight ahead at a cross-track a few yards further on. Where the track joins a fence it peters out. Continue with the fence to your left to the corner of a small wood which can be seen ahead. Note the ridge and furrow evidence here of former ploughland. Bearing right, continue with the fence on your left to another small plantation. Marshy land and a pond lie to the right. Continue past the wood over a rise. The track is grassed over, but the route should be evident. Over to the left can be seen the pond of a former water mill.

The path meets a surfaced track. Turn right and walk along the track. As we near the Old Hall, we pass (on the left) the site of a longhouse possibly of the Roman period, the site of the medieval village devastated by the Black Death, and the grassed hollow of the old "Portstreet" to Knutsford. To the right lay extensive open field ploughlands. Wooden structures enclose information boards. It is worth allowing time to wander around this area.

A track on the left leads to the Old Hall, the oldest parts of which were built around 1460. When the first of the succession of new halls was built on the other side of the park, probably in the late seventeenth century, the Old Hall was inhabited by estate tenants, and later by estate servants.

Our route continues ahead past the Old Hall. The track is now a tarred drive: follow it down to a junction between the meres. Turn left, then right onto a track beside Tatton Mere, which is to your left. A field path follows the mereside to a gate in a fence; beyond this the faintly visible path crosses fields to enter woodland. A track is joined, and leads to a wooden park boundary gate somewhat less grand than our point of entry. Go through the gate, and follow the track through Dog Wood until you come to a bridge over the railway. Here you can continue ahead on a rather rough but well-used unofficial path through Knutsford Moor (a former common) until you emerge beyond a pumping station onto a park. Turn right onto the path which crosses the front of the Moor Pool. Continue ahead and you will emerge onto King Street. Turn left to return to the railway station. You can hardly fail to notice Watt's Gaskell Memorial Tower and Coffee House (1907-8).

Toward the end of King Street, the station approach is to the right before the railway bridge. But if you wish to see the Unitarian Chapel of 1689, where Mrs Gaskell is buried, go under the bridge. The chapel lies on the other side of the main road.

1. THE SESSIONS HOUSE

Knutsford, surrounded by a remarkable number of the "seats" of the county gentry, had become by the late 18th century the

social powerhouse of central and eastern Cheshire. Aiken in 1795 mentioned the elegant assembly room, and races "inferior to few in the kingdom for display of fashionable company." At Knutsford the gentry exercised its administrative and judicial power at Quarter Sessions; the facade of the Sessions House of 1818 must have been deliberately designed as the visible expression of that power. Here also sat the County Court, and the Crown Court still sits here.

Behind the Sessions House, on a four acre site surrounded by a high brick wall, was a County House of Correction, a prison complete with whipping posts, "dark cells" for the refractory, and treadmills (which pumped water for the prison). Bagshaw's Cheshire Directory of 1850 described the prison in detail, with evident admiration. A central building housed the offices of the governor and chaplain. Of the four radiating wings, one was allocated to female prisoners. Some of the 700 or so prisoners were held "on the separate system", some having hand looms in their cells; others associated together in their work and at mealtimes. The prisoners were classified, and their diet varied. Most were class five: their food consisted of a pint of cocoa and 6oz of bread for breakfast, a pint of soup, 16oz of potatoes, 3oz of meat, and 6oz of bread for dinner, and 6oz of bread and a pint of gruel for supper.

Printed calendars outline the fate in prison of those convicted at the Quarter Sessions. At the May sessions of 1843, for instance, Robert Brown (24) got four months hard labour for stealing a duck; George Spruce (15) was to get six months hard labour and two whippings for stealing 3 lbs of tobacco; Maria Cookson (16), Phoebe Hamlet (16) and Thomas Hamlet

(11) each received one month hard labour for stealing 2cwt of coal.

By 1914, Knutsford prison no longer took criminal prisoners. During the first world war it housed conscientious objectors and prisoners of war. For a few years after the war former servicemen trained here for ordination in the Church of England. The former prison was demolished in the 1930s.

2. HIGHWAYMAN HIGGINS

Highwayman Higgins lived, it is believed, in a house on the site of Heath House in Gaskell Avenue for perhaps eight or nine years between the mid 1750s and the mid 1760s. He was hanged at Carmarthen in 1767. Ever since, Higgins seems to have been considered an adornment of Knutsford's history, rather than a blot on it.

The highwaymen of the eighteenth century often became popular heroes, due to a variety of supposed characteristics. They were thought to be courteous and chivalrous, sometimes from "good" families; they were handsome, strong, clever; they were skilled horsemen and swordsmen. Elegant and subversive, they were seen to challenge and to mock respectable high society.

How does Knutsford's highwayman measure up? Higgins' body was apparently "manufactured into a skeleton" by the famous surgeon Cruikshank, and ended up in the museum of Mr White of Manchester. De Quincey, who saw it there, described it as "superb looking". Clever and bold Higgins must have been: before he came to Knutsford he had been convicted of a robbery and transported to Maryland, where he quickly

Highwayman Higgins' house

committed another robbery, and made his way home on the proceeds.

In Knutsford, Higgins married well, had five children, and is said to have "made himself popular among the kind hearted rustics by his general courtesy." He lived as a gentleman. In the words of Henry Green (*Knutsford, Its Traditions and History*, 1869), he was "on visiting terms, as well as housebreaking terms, with the neighbouring gentry. He hunted with them in the morning, dined with them in the afternoon, and made himself familiar with their plate-chests by night."

The unromantic truth seems to be that Higgins was a house-breaker, often using the highways to roam widely for plunder, on expeditions which he later explained to his wife as journeys to collect rents from scattered estates. One robbery at least involved a brutal murder – that of an old woman and her female servant in Bristol. This much Higgins confessed in a letter which he gave to the Sheriff as he mounted the ladder to the gallows, having failed by a hair's breadth to secure his own escape with a reprieve forged by an accomplice.

3. TATTON PARK.

Tatton Park, which passed to the National Trust in 1958, is now a superb leisure facility: thousands of acres of undulating naturalistic landscape forming an enclave for the public in the busy farmland of central Cheshire. But it is worth remembering that this naturally well-drained land was once also farmed and settled, and that it was ruthlessly and systematically cleared in the 18th century by the Egerton family of Tatton Hall, for nobody's enjoyment but their own.

An estate map of 1733 shows two settlements within the present park boundary: Tatton village, around the Old Hall, and Norshaw near Birkin Heath to the north. Tatton village had been settled continuously since at least Saxon times, and people had farmed there as long as 5,000 years ago. By the late seventeenth century, the population consisted of perhaps around thirty five families. Arable farming was the mainstay of the community. The old open fields had been enclosed. Occupations such as carpenter, fuller, tailor, blacksmith, and innkeeper appear in the parish records.

Clearance took place between the 1750s and the 1780s. Leases were not renewed, or were bought out. Tenants appear to have been given some time to find alternative accommodation, and some were rehoused in Knutsford or Rostherne. Houses, farms, hedges and barns were torn down. Only the Old Hall was retained, divided into apartments for estate servants.

Landscape architects were brought in. William Eames (1766), Humphry Repton (1791), and John Webb (c.1816-18) all contributed to the design of the park. The purpose of the park was to enhance the hall, and the status of the Egertons, but some agricultural use was retained: from the 1780s the park grassland served as a ley for local farmers' cattle. Ordinary folk, however, got scarcely a glimpse inside. Fletcher Moss, the Didsbury antiquarian, wrote in 1910 that "Tatton Park is an immense place, kept private most rigidly and rigorously ... it is said to be eleven miles around, and has twenty six locked gates." LE

the Tatton Gate, Knutsford

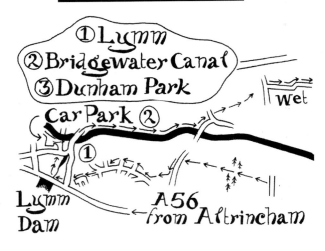

① Lymm
② Bridgewater Canal
③ Dunham Park
Car Park ②
①
wet
Lymm
Dam
A56
from Altrincham

Lymm to Dunham

LENGTH OF WALK: The circular walk is approximately eight miles long. An extension of half a mile at Little Bollington will take you into Dunham Park.

DEGREE OF DIFFICULTY: Low.

PUBLIC TRANSPORT: Bus services to Lymm, where this walk starts, are available from Warrington, Altrincham and Knutsford.

ORDNANCE SURVEY MAP: At 1:25,000, this walk can be found on Pathfinder map 740 (Warrington).

This walk along the gentle slopes of the southern side of the Mersey valley begins in the picturesque village of Lymm, where cottages, shops and inns crowd into a narrow wooded ravine. We strike eastwards along the towpath of the Bridgewater Canal, before taking to the fields at Oughtrington, and crossing the River Bollin near Wet Gate Farm. The field beyond the river can be quite muddy in wet weather – stout boots are required. After a short stretch along a disused railway, our route lies through the fields of the Bollin valley to Little Bollington, which is adjacent to Dunham Park and Dunham Massey Hall.

We return to Lymm along another stretch of the Bridgewater Canal, which follows a circuitous course around the contours of the valley, and then by field paths (which can get muddy in places), emerging at the parish church which stands above Lymm Dam, an artificial lake created to supply water to the mills in the valley below. We return to the village centre through "the Dingle", shaded by woods between sandstone cliffs.

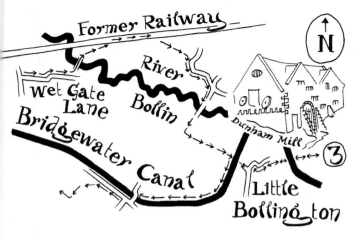

This walk begins near the centre of the village of **Lymm (1)**, at the
Bridgewater Canal (2). A free car park is available next to the
canal, off Bridgewater Street. Walk out of the car park direct onto
the canalside path, and cross the aqueduct. The Lymm corn mill
was situated in the valley on the right; the slitting mill was further
downstream on the other (towpath) side of the aqueduct.

Walk to the road bridge which you can see ahead, cross over, and
continue ahead along the towpath for about a mile. The next over-
bridge is at the village of Oughtrington. Leave the canal here, and
follow the road to the left. Where the road twists sharply leftwards,
carry straight on along a footpath which passes between houses and
then crosses a field in the direction of Heatley. The pool visible to
the left is a subsidence "flash" caused by the extraction of brine.
Rock salt and brine were discovered in Heatley and Agden around
1901. In the area to the left of the flash, Charles Moore and Co.
operated a saltworks where the famous "Lymm Pure Salt" was
produced. The works closed in the 1950s.

Continue along the field path to Mill Lane. Turn left, then
immediately right into Wet Gate Lane. This name, very appropriate
in the days before the channel of the River Bollin was embanked,
means "allotments of damp pasture land." Follow the quiet lane,
continuing for a few hundred yards past Wet Gate Farm, and then
take the waymarked track on the left which leads to a bridge across
the Bollin. Over the bridge, take the path signed to Warburton,
which crosses the field, making for the railway embankment. The
mud here can be very sticky in wet weather.

Walk up to the trackbed of the former Warrington and Stockport
Railway, and continue ahead. This line, opened in 1853, was closed
for passengers in 1962, and for freight in 1986. Walk along the
railway for a few hundred yards to the next path on the right,
signed to Dunham Woodhouses. Walk along this path through fields

61

to Barns Lane, turn right and walk to the small village of Dunham Woodhouses. Where Barns Lane meets Woodhouse Lane, carry straight on for a few yards, then turn right into Meadow Lane, which is really just a track leading down to a bridge over the Bollin.

Over the bridge, cross the stile and carry on across the field. A ditch is crossed by a footbridge. Walk up the bank beyond to a stile, and carry on across the next field as far as a guidepost, which is in the middle of the field. Here make a right angle turn leftwards, and walk to a stile. Beyond, carry straight on, with the hedge on your right. Pass a small wood, then carry straight on across a field following the slightly raised but completely grassed over line of a former track. In the corner of the field beyond the pylon, go through the gate and follow the grassed over track down to the canal embankment.

Our way back to Lymm lies to the right, along the canal towpath. However, if you wish to go into **Dunham Park (3)**, or just look at it from Little Bollington, continue along the track under the canal. Beyond, a cobbled lane leads to the village, where it joins a tarred road. Turn left here, and walk past the Swan With Two Nicks (food available) down to a footbridge over the Bollin. A large former corn mill is on the left; the path beyond the bridge crosses the leat which brought water to the wheel. The path leads directly across a field to the park and hall which can be seen ahead.

Return from the park to the Bridgewater Canal by the same route. Pass under the canal, turn left to gain access to the towpath, and continue ahead for about a mile. At the next over-bridge (Agden Bridge) leave the towpath. Use the bridge to cross the canal, and turn right at the road junction. It is necessary now to walk for about 400 yards along Warrington Lane which runs alongside the canal. Be careful: this road can be quite busy, and the verges are narrow.

Take the waymarked field path on the left. This crosses the field diagonally to a stile, which is marked by a tall post. Across the stile, turn left and follow the hedgerow to the top of the field, then turn right and follow the hedgerows straight on through the fields to Burford Lane. This stretch can be very muddy indeed; but you do get an interesting view across the Mersey valley from this slight prominence.

At Burford Lane turn right, then after a few yards take the field path on the left. Helsdale Wood lies ahead. The path skirts a former sandstone quarry, now flooded by a blocked stream, before entering the wood. Beyond, follow the path straight on alongside a fence, past Lymm High School (formerly Lymm Grammar School, which liked to trace its origins back to around 1600) to Oughtrington Lane. Turn left, and walk past St Peter's Church, built 1871-2. I find the blackened stone and sharp spire rather impressive, but Pevsner says "not a satisfactory church."

Take the waymarked path on the right, which crosses a field between fences and emerges near to a junction of roads. Take the quiet lane on the right, and follow this straight across two new estate roads to the point where three ways diverge. Take the tarmac path on the left, which rises above Longbutt Lane. Follow this straight on toward the tower of Lymm church, with houses on the left and a playing field on the right. Where the path ends, continue ahead along a stretch of suburban road, at the end of which a short path leads to the main road at Church Green, in front of the parish church. The original Anglo Saxon village of Lymm may have been situated in this area. Turn right, but ignore Rectory Lane which is immediately to the right and marked "to the village". Instead follow Church Road – the main road – across the front of Lymm Dam. There was only a footbridge here before the construction of the Stockton Heath to Stockport turnpike road around 1823. Steps on the right lead down to a track through the Dingle, which emerges in the village centre by the Lower Dam pool. To see Lymm Cross (probably seventeenth century) turn right; to return directly to the car park turn left, then right.

1. LYMM

The Anglo Saxon village of Lymm may have derived its name from the Old English word for the sound of the rushing water which would have been heard in Lymm Hollow. Since then, the gorge has been widened by sandstone quarrying, and the stream has been dammed at various points to provide power for water mills.

A corn mill formerly stood in the centre of the village, across the road from the Lower Dam. It is said to have been driven by a wooden undershot wheel. The mill was demolished around 1935 for road widening.

Further downstream, below the aqueduct of the Bridgewater Canal, a slitting mill had been erected by the early years of the eighteenth century. Here iron bars were rolled into sheets, then cut into strips to make barrel hoops and nails. Presumably, the iron was brought to the site by the River Mersey, and perhaps up the

Lymm Dam

local Sow Brook. The site was disused by the 1830s, but traces of the water power arrangements remain.

Lymm did not develop into a modern industrial town as the water power potential was too limited, and the site too constricted. In the mid-nineteenth century the majority of the population were still agricultural workers, but there was a considerable number of fustian cutters (720 in 1862). Manchester manufacturers sent cotton twill to Lymm to be turned into velveteen or corduroy by the cutters, who were employed on piece rates by local "putters-out".

The cutting was done by hand: a highly skilled job, and a physically stressful one, as the worker had to constantly bend sideways to the right over the cutting frame, in the close and dusty atmosphere of a small workshop or garret. Children would be started on the work full time at the age of eight or nine. Dr. Henry Simpson described the physical consequences before the Royal Commission on Childrens' Employment, which took evidence in Lymm in 1862. Many of the cutters were "pale looking and diminutive ... defect of figure is very conspicuous and prevalent; the distortion inwards of the right knee is most so ... the high shoulder, which is another deformity amongst cutters, if it were an aggravated form, would be accompanied by distortion of the spine."

Hardly surprising perhaps that the fustian cutters "crave for the excitement of drinking; most of their houses are dirty and uncomfortable, their children dirty and ill brought up." Unsurprising too that the cutters clung to the one benefit of this type of employment – "the masters have tried to enforce fixed hours, but the workers have been too strong for them: they will be irregular, and take their Monday and Tuesday too for play days."

2. BRIDGEWATER CANAL

The Bridgewater Canal was the first English 'dead water' canal, entirely independent of rivers, and so can be said to have ushered in the 'canal age' during which Britain's industrial revolution was facilitated and stimulated by the construction of a national network of trunk canals. The first stage of the canal, which was completed by 1763, linked Manchester with the Duke of Bridgewater's coal mines at Worsley. The canal, which was engineered by the Duke's agent John Gilbert and the semi-literate genius James Brindley, actually emerged from the underground waterways of the mines themselves.

The second stage of the canal left the original line at Stretford, crossed the Mersey, and followed the south side of the Mersey valley through Altrincham (reached by 1766), Lymm (reached by 1769) and on to the Mersey at Runcorn, to provide access to Liverpool. The whole canal was open by 1776, by which time the Trent and Mersey Canal formed a southward link from Preston Brook.

The Duke's canal succeeded in providing cheaper coal for Manchester and the westward districts, and it brought agricultural produce, salt, and a wide range of merchandise eastwards. A passenger service was introduced as early as 1766, between Manchester and Lymm. As the fast passenger services were run by

the Duke's estate, they were given priority on the canal. The passenger boats carried a curved knife mounted on the bow to cut the tow ropes of boats which didn't give way.

Lewis's Directory of 1788 described the two "elegant passage-boats, for Passengers and their Luggage only." The west-bound boat "leaves Manchester every morning at eight o'clock, except Saturday, and on that day at four in the afternoon; passes Altringham [sic] about ten o'clock; Lymm at half past eleven; Warrington at one o'clock, where the Liverpool coach meets it ... and arrives at Runcorn at half past four in the evening." On this, and on the equivalent east-bound service, "tea and cakes are elegantly served for breakfast, and in the afternoons."

3. DUNHAM PARK

Dunham Massey and its estate have been in the hands of only three families for almost all of the second millennium. The Masseys held it at the time of the Domesday Book (1086) and down to 1342. The head of each of the six known generations was called Hamo. From the early 15th century to the mid-eighteenth, the Booth family held Dunham Massey. They were succeeded by the Earls of Stamford. When the 10th Earl died in 1976, the house, park, and the remaining estate passed to the National Trust.

Parts of the splendid park have long been open to the public – since the late eighteenth century, probably. The park and hall as they stand today are essentially the work of George Booth, 2nd Earl of Warrington (1675-1758), who turned his back on the turbulent politics and expensive court life of his ancestors, and restored the family finances by arranging a marriage for himself to Mary Oldbury, the daughter of a wealthy London merchant. The second Earl was a man of ferocious temper. He quarrelled with his wife, and they lived in the house "as absolute strangers to each other at bed and board." But he used her money to rebuild the hall, and to plant around it 100,000 oaks, elms and beeches, with five main avenues radiating from the house. Figueiredo and Treuherz describe the park as "one of the most ambitious formal parks in the north west" (*Cheshire Country Houses*, 1988). Cheap passenger services on the Bridgewater Canal, which lies to the north of the park, provided access for visitors from the industrial areas. "The grounds are much frequented by parties from Manchester and its neighbourhood" stated the entry in Pigot's 1834 Directory. "Joyous groups may be seen, on a summer's day, solacing themselves on the verdant sward, beneath the umbrageous foliage, or rambling amid the cool recesses of this truly sylvan scenery." The Directory added, more prosaically, that the Dog i' th' Wall in the nearby village could provide refreshment for "holiday visiters" [sic]. Visitors continued to arrive at Dunham Park by canal until the First World War. **LE**

the mill at Dunham Massey

Macclesfield to Langley

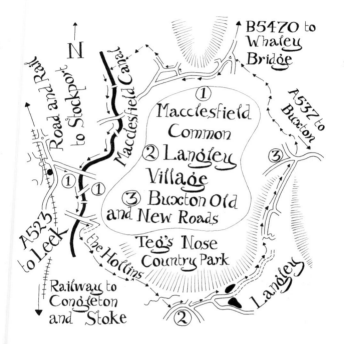

LENGTH OF WALK: Approximately nine and a half miles (starting and finishing at Macclesfield Station) or approximately eight and a half miles (starting and finishing at Buxton Road canal bridge).

DIFFICULTY RATING: Low/medium.

ORDNANCE SURVEY MAP: At 1:25,000, this walk can be found on Pathfinder map 759 (Macclesfield and Alderley Edge).

PUBLIC TRANSPORT: Macclesfield is on the railway line from Stockport and Manchester to Congleton and Stoke. Bus services come to Macclesfield from Leek, Sandbach and Congleton, Alderley Edge and Wilmslow, Poynton and Stockport, New Mills and Whaley Bridge, and Buxton.

This walk begins at Macclesfield railway station, but if you come by car you may wish to park near Buxton Road canal bridge, and start and finish the walk from there. After a short stretch on the canal towpath, we walk over the Hollins by field paths to the rural mill village of Langley, above which looms the rocky quarry-spoil face of Tegg's Nose.

An old packhorse trail is followed up to the Setter Dog Inn at Walker Barn, where the old and new Buxton roads from

*Macclesfield meet. We walk along the edge of a beautiful
amphitheatre in the hills, in which the villages of Rainow and
Bollington nestle, before walking down to the gap at Kerridge End
which gives access to the lowlands. In Swanscoe fields we see
evidence of early coal mining before we return to the starting point
along the towpath of the contour-hugging Macclesfield Canal.*

Turn right as you leave Macclesfield Station, and right again to
pass under the railway bridge. This first part of the walk climbs up
through **Macclesfield Common (1).** Cross the busy inner by-pass
at the traffic lights, and walk up Buxton Road to the bridge over the
Macclesfield Canal. At the bottom of the canal access steps, turn left
and follow the towpath under the bridge and past the former Hovis
Mill (on the right). Continue along the towpath for half a mile or so,
to bridge 40.

Climb the steps up to the road, and turn left up the hill. After a
few yards Blakelow Road swings left. Here, carry straight on, up
Hollins Road. After a right angle bend to the right there are good
panoramic views across Macclesfield.

Carry straight on past the golf club entrance, but after a few
yards take the path through the wall on the left. Ignore gates to the
left and then to the right which lead on to the golf course. On a
slight rise, cross over a stone track and continue ahead. At the top
of the field cross the stone track again, and then take the upper
path, which continues along the contour of the hill, with the golf
course on the left.

A stile leads into an open field, where the path is not distinct.
Carry straight on, skirting the gorse bushes which lie in the way. To
the right you now see the village of Sutton, with St. James's Church
standing above it. Continue over a brow, and you will be able to see
the path which passes along the hillside just below the bracken and
gorse. The path runs by the remains of a stone wall, and traces of
stone surfacing can be seen: this path was once very well used, as
the quickest way between Macclesfield and Langley (which can
soon be seen ahead).

The path emerges from gorse bushes at a small valley. Cross the
stream, and turn right to walk down to Langley. A waymarked stile
below the first field shows the way. The River Bollin is crossed by a
footbridge. At the top of the riverbank, cross the field and follow a
stone wall up to the Langley road.

Turn left and walk along the roadside footpath into **Langley
Village (2).** Langley Hall is on the left after a few yards, and
beyond that is the Langley Institute. Carry on up to the Wesleyan
chapel, then turn left along Main Road. A few hundred yards
further on, turn left into Holehurst Lane. Stag Hollow on the left
occupies the site of the Bollinhead Mills, which were probably the
first mills in Langley.

The raised garden behind is the site of the mill pool. Another pool
lies further up, on the right, below the embankment of Bottoms
Reservoir (opened in 1850). Follow the road past the parking space
at the top of the hill, keeping to the right. Continue along what is

now a stone track. Below Tegg's Nose, on the left, is Teggsnose Reservoir (opened 1870). Bottoms and Teggsnose Reservoirs are both compensation reservoirs: Ridgegate (1850) and Trentabank (1929) further upstream supply water to Macclesfield.

After about half a mile the track forks. Bear left, walk down to the stream and up the wide steps on the other side. Through a gate, a former packhorse trail leads along the valley side. This joins a narrow, quiet lane: continue up the valley along this lane for about three quarters of a mile, until it joins the main Buxton road just above the Setter Dog Inn at Walker Barn. **Below the Setter Barn, the old and new Buxton Roads (3)** separate.

Cross the wall on the opposite side of the main road by the wooden steps, and walk down into the valley. Where the track swings to the right, continue straight down to the causeway over the stream. This quite substantial feature now leads nowhere. We are following what appears to be a lost road from Walker Barn to Horderne Farm and Rainow. Across the stream, follow the path on the left along the valley side and round the hill to Horderne Farm (which was really a small settlement). Walk straight on between the buildings, and continue along the fenced track beyond.

At the crest of the hill we see Rainow and in the distance Bollington, encircled by hills. White Nancy, a whitewashed sugar-loaf folly, gleams at the far end of the hogsback ridge of Kerridge Hill. Walk down the track for a few yards, then take the waymarked path on the left. Cross the metal stile and walk straight on, following the wall. Across the valley to the right can be seen The Oaks, one of the few remaining patches of relict wildwood in the Peak.

A green lane leads up a small hill. Just before the top, climb the wooden stile on the left. The path beyond is not clear. Swing rightwards around the knoll, and then cross the field toward the wall ahead, then walk down to the cottages at Brookhouse which you can see ahead. Turn right onto the lane, then left onto the main road (the former Macclesfield-Fernilee turnpike road, authorised in 1770).

We must now follow the road up to the gap of Kerridge End, and then down to Cesterbridge – a distance of just over half a mile, but with a path all the way. Where the road levels out, turn right off the main road into Kerridge Road, then left into Swanscoe Lane. Carry straight on where another lane joins from the left (note the fenced-off coal mine shaft), and where a private road branches off to the right. Pass through the gateway of Shrigley Fold, then take the track on the right to by-pass the buildings. Where the track swings round into a farmyard, carry straight on. Another track is joined, which leads down into a hollow.

The next stretch can be rather muddy in wet weather. Turn left into the field before a rise with an old stone barn at the top. The path is not waymarked. It follows ruts which run along slightly raised ground in a straight line up to the trees of a former hedgerow. Note the coal mining hummocks on the right.

At the trees, continue ahead, bearing slightly to the left. A waymarked stile leads to a plank bridge over a stream. On the other side, turn right, cross another stile, then turn left. Over the next stile swing right and cross the field diagonally towards the silver sheds of the AstraZeneca works at Hursdfield. We join the canal towpath at the site of a former swingbridge. Turn left and follow the towpath back to Buxton Road bridge – a distance of just over a mile.

1. MACCLESFIELD COMMON

Macclesfield Common stretched from the Waters (the area around the railway station) all the way up to what is now Tegg's Nose Country Park. For the most part, the Common presented a wild, partly wooded, and unkempt face to the town. But the Common was not waste. The owners of properties in Macclesfield could use

the former Hovis mill

the land to graze animals, gather wood and food, and get stone.

In 1796, the process of enclosure began. The Enclosure Act of that year noted that there had already been many "encroachments and inclosures taken from and made upon the said commons... whereupon messuages, shops, mills, warehouses and other buildings are now erected and standing." This development had taken place at the bottom of the Common, close to the river. Higher up, the Mayor and Corporation were exercising the right given them by the charter of 1684 to build reservoirs to supply Macclesfield with water by means of "certain pipes, conduits or tunnels of wood heretofore sunk." The act also mentioned "pits, shafts, levels, soughs, tunnels, machines and engines" which were used to mine the various seams of "coal, cannel, and slack" which lay under the Common.

Enclosure was inspired by high food prices and the rapid growth of Macclesfield's silk industry which occurred during the French Wars, from 1793. The Corporation and other owners of common rights were over-optimistic, envisaging houses and small farms all the way up Buxton Road. Some of the roads laid out at the top end of the Common remain as unused green lanes today.

An important stimulus to the development of the lower part of the Common came in 1831 with the opening of the Macclesfield Canal, which crossed Buxton Road at a distance of half a mile from the town. Goods were loaded and unloaded at the nearby wharves. The Puss in Boots Inn became, briefly, an interchange point for businessmen and socialites arriving by 'swift packet boat' from Bollington who wished to travel on to the delights of Buxton by coach.

2. LANGLEY VILLAGE

Langley was almost entirely rural before the Industrial Revolution. Thus Langley Hall could be advertised in the *Manchester Mercury* in 1793 as "a capital mansion, fit for the immediate reception of a genteel family." There were gardens and pleasure grounds, and the

three streams which ran through the estate were "abounding with trout."

The advertisement for the Hall also suggested that manufacturers might find the streams suitable for powering water wheels. David Yates, who bought the estate, lost little time in establishing silk mills upstream of the Hall. By 1850, according to Bagshaw's *Cheshire Directory*, Langley was home to bleaching, silk throwing, silk dyeing, silk printing and smallware manufacturing businesses. Industrial premises and terraced housing had closed in around the Hall, which had been divided into several tenements and was in a miserable state of repair.

Industrial Langley was not a planned community: the terraced housing of the early nineteenth century, such as that along Main Road, 'just growed'. But the manufacturers, from Yates onwards, encouraged the Methodism which took hold in industrial areas more easily than attendance at the established church. Services were at first held in a barn behind Langley Hall. Isaac Smith, Yates's successor, financed the first Wesleyan chapel, which was built in 1818. Later manufacturers, all of them nonconformist and Liberal, encouraged and supported the setting up of a mechanics' institute, reading rooms, and eventually the Institute which was opened in 1883 and extended in 1911. A school (the present Education Centre) was opened in 1877.

For those Langley folk who were not entirely occupied by self-improvement, and there may have been some, the St. Dunstan Inn on Main Road was first licensed in 1825.

3. BUXTON OLD AND NEW ROADS

As trade grew in the eighteenth century, many main roads were turnpiked: tolls levied on traffic financed improvements and better maintenance. What is now referred to as the old Buxton road was the first of Macclesfield's roads to be turnpiked, after an Act of 1758. Like most early turnpikes, it followed an existing route which avoided marshy valley floors as much as possible, and tackled hills head on, with steep gradients. Later turnpikes, such as the 'new' Buxton road, opened in 1823, followed gentler though longer routes around the contours of hills, which made heavier loads possible for horse-drawn traffic.

The old and new Buxton roads converged for a short distance at the tiny hamlet of Walker Barn, which was the site of a toll bar. The Setter Dog Inn which stands here has a 1740 datestone, and so the inn may predate the first turnpike. Its early name, the Pack Horse, may reflect the type of traffic which passed by, or it may be derived from a carrying business run by the landlord. In the nineteenth century the name of the inn changed to the Dog and Gun, then the Dog and Partridge. By 1869, when Jonathan Longden took over the license, the present name had been adopted.

Roads such as these, with long isolated stretches, were dangerous for travellers. In 1815 the editor of the *Macclesfield Courier* warned country people that they should return from market with friends, as robberies were so frequent. The paper carried an account of a close shave experienced in 1848, not far from Walker Barn, by Mr Caldwell of Knutsford, who was travelling on horseback to Buxton. In the pouring rain, he encountered six men walking abreast. Caldwell described them as "all Irishmen, of rough ferocious appearance ... each being furnished with a stout rough shillelagh." As he squeezed between them, two of the men seized the bridle, demanded money, and when refused began to swear and threaten. Caldwell was saved at the last minute by the appearance of other travellers in the distance, at which the alleged Irishmen cleared off over the walls on either side of the road. **LE**

The Setter Dog, where old and new Buxton roads meet

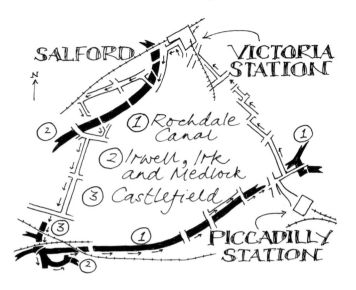

LivingEDGE Walk No. 11

Manchester City Centre

SALFORD   VICTORIA STATION

N

① Rochdale Canal
② Irwell, Irk and Medlock
③ Castlefield

PICCADILLY STATION

LENGTH OF WALK: about three and a half miles.

DEGREE OF DIFFICULTY: easy.

PUBLIC TRANSPORT: this walk begins at Manchester Piccadilly railway station, which is served by the Hadfield, Hope Valley, Buxton, Stoke, Crewe, Styal, and Chester (via Knutsford) lines, as well as by trains from Warrington and by Metrolink trams from Altrincham.

ORDNANCE SURVEY MAP: At 1:25000 this walk can be found on Pathfinder map 724 (Manchester and Ashton-Under-Lyne), but for this walk, a larger scale A-Z street map would be more useful.

This walk is a circuit of the outer city centre of Manchester, focusing on the waterways which helped to establish Manchester as a commercial and industrial centre. Close by Piccadilly Station we look at the former wharves of the Rochdale and Ashton Canals. We walk through the warehouse and market districts down to Victoria Station, where the hidden River Irk joins the River Irwell. Crossing Victoria Bridge we pass briefly into Salford, returning to Manchester over an elegant new suspension footbridge. At Castlefield Urban Park, we walk by the waters of the country's first real canal, the Bridgewater Canal, up to the River Medlock which feeds it. We return to Piccadilly Station alongside the locks of the Rochdale Canal, in its urban canyon.

We begin this walk with the assumption that you have arrived in Manchester by train, at Piccadilly Station. At the bottom of the station approach, turn right into Ducie Street. On the right is a former railway warehouse, built in the 1860s (when the original London Road Station of 1842 was rebuilt).

Next left is Dale Street. The Dale Street car park, through a castellated archway, is on the site of the basin of the **Rochdale Canal (1)**. Our route lies along Dale Street; but if you first walk up the right hand side of Ducie Street, after a few yards you can see on the right the former basin of the Ashton Canal. A link under Ducie Street connects it with the Rochdale Canal. Cross over Ducie Street and return to Dale Street; on the way you can look over the Dale Street basin and see two canal warehouses of the early 19th century, one in brick and one in stone.

Walk along Dale Street past the entrance to the canal basin, and on into the district of commercial warehouses. Textile warehouses have been described as "Manchester's pre-eminent building type, peculiar to the city and its mercantile development." The grandest warehouses, such as that now occupied by the Britannia Hotel, lie closer to the city centre but the Dale Street area retains more of the atmosphere of the city which I remember from my childhood in the 1950s.

Continue along Dale Street, past the intersection with Newton Street. Turn right into Lever Street, then turn left at Stevenson Square, and walk ahead down Hilton Street. Turn right into Oak Street, then left into Copperas Street, immediately in front of the Manchester Craft and Design Centre.

We are now in the area where Manchester's markets were concentrated in the 19th century. (Manchester had been a market town from at least the 13th century; the original market place was probably in the area now occupied by Marks and Spencers, at the bottom of Market Street.) Smithfield market was to the right of Copperas Street – across the car park is a stone hall erected by Manchester Corporation in 1857. Ahead are the red brick walls of the wholesale fish market building opened in 1873.

At the end of Copperas Street, walk ahead along the path through the former market area. At the road beyond (Shude Hill) turn left, then right, following the roads by the tram tracks down to Victoria Station.

Walk along the early 20th century station front. Inside the third entrance way is a huge tile map showing the empire of the Lancashire and Yorkshire Railway at its height. Part of the original station (built in 1844 on Hunt's Bank) survives, where the road swings round to the left. Follow the road. Below on the left is Walker's Croft, beneath which is the culverted **River Irk (2)**. Beyond, once high on the river bank, are mediaeval buildings which became incorporated in Chetham's School (founded 1653).

At the bottom of the station approach is Victoria Street. Cross over (with great caution). **The River Irwell (2)** is on the other side of the stone wall. Turn left. If you enter the car park on the right and look back through the railings you will see the entrance to the tunnel which brings the Irk into the Irwell.

The bridge over the Irwell at this point was rebuilt by Salford Corporation in 1912. Do not cross the river here; carry on along Victoria Street. The next bridge across the Irwell led only to Exchange Station (opened 1884; closed 1969). We cross the Irwell on the bridge beyond, Victoria Bridge, built on what seems to have been the earliest bridging point between Manchester and Salford. The present bridge was opened in the year of Victoria"s coronation, 1838. From the parapet you can see, downstream, Blackfriars Bridge (opened 1820, replacing a wooden footbridge).

Turn left into Chapel Street. Carry on across the intersection with Blackfriars Road. On the right is the church of Sacred Trinity (founded 1653; rebuilt 1753). Walk right up to the railway bridge ahead. Turn left after the bus shelter and walk up to and across the elegant new suspension footbridge across the Irwell, next to Manchester's new five-star hotel – the Lowry.

Turn right at the top of the bridge approach, and right again on to Bridge Street, which leads down to Albert Bridge (formerly New Bailey Bridge, built c. 1785; rebuilt 1844). Our route lies along Gartside Street, on the left; but on the riverbank beyond is the Pump House People's History Museum, formerly one of three municipal pumping stations which provided a supply of hydraulic power through high pressure mains beneath the streets which was widely used in the city's warehouses. An entrance fee is charged – but not for the shop and café.

We now walk straight ahead for about a third of a mile, along Gartside Street, then along Lower Byrom Street, up to Liverpool Road. Here, the Museum of Science and Industry, on the right, occupies former railway warehouses. On the left, Lower Campfield market hall (1876) has become the museum's Air and Space Hall.

Turn right on to Liverpool Road. Our route lies to the left, just past the Castlefield Centre, where steps lead down to the **Castlefield Canal Basin (3)**. But a little further down Liverpool Road, on the right, are the buildings of the world's first passenger station which was opened in 1830 at the terminus of the Liverpool and Manchester Railway. The station was never rebuilt as it became a goods depot in 1844 when the line was diverted to Hunt's Bank and Victoria Station opened.

Go down the steps from the Castlefield Centre and walk along the left side of the wharves. We pass under a low brick railway viaduct, then after a short canal side walk under two high iron viaducts,with a footbridge over a canal arm in between, and then under another low brick viaduct. The brick bridges were opened by the Manchester and Altrincham Railway Company in 1849 (the first being a link to the Liverpool line); the first of the iron bridges was opened in 1864, the second in 1877, providing access to the Great Northern Railway Warehouse and to Central Station (now G-Mex) respectively.

Cross the Bridgewater Canal by the curving modern footbridge, and then follow the canal to the left. The entrance to the Rochdale Canal and the Merchant's Warehouse (circa 1823) are across the canal on the left; ahead is the Middle Warehouse (1831), now called Castle Quay. Cross the footbridge in front of Castle Quay, and continue alongside the Bridgewater Canal.

The original coal wharves were situated on the other side of the canal. Cross the next footbridge. To the right, the **River Medlock (2)** feeds into the Bridgewater Canal. Climb the stairs next to the reconstructed Grocers Warehouse on the left. Cross the stone-paved street and go down the ramp to the towpath of the Rochdale Canal. The original canal tunnel at this point was opened out in 1849, when the railway was built.

Turn right onto the towpath. We now follow the canal as it skirts the city centre, passing under Deansgate and Oxford Road. The Rochdale Canal passes through nine locks between Castlefield and the Dale Street basin. Just after Tib Lock (no. 89) evidence can be seen of an old canal arm which led to the Manchester and Salford Junction Canal (1839), which formed a link (largely underground) with the River Irwell.

After lock 87, we go up to Princess Street, and turn right, then right again into Canal Street, which runs alongside the canal, and served as the towpath. At Minshull Street, cross the canal, turn sharp left and return to Piccadilly Station, which can be seen ahead.

1. ROCHDALE CANAL

The Rochdale Canal runs through central Manchester in dark canyons between warehouses and offices, from the Bridgewater Canal basin at Castlefield to its own former wharves and offices in Dale Street, near Piccadilly, before striking out for Rochdale and then climbing over the Pennines to join the eastern waterway system at Sowerby Bridge – 33 miles in all, with 92 locks.

The Rochdale Canal, the first trans-Pennine waterway, was fully opened in December 1804, and opened in some style, according to the *Morning Chronicle*. "The bells of Manchester commenced ringing at half past two, and the company's passage boat and yacht, the Saville and the Travis, were greeted from the banks for a great distance by an immense concourse of spectators, with many a vociferous cheer... each gentleman [on the boats], together with every servant and workman of the company, wore in his hat a blue ribbon, with the inscription in gold letters – *Success to the Rochdale Canal.*"

Successful the Rochdale Canal was, until the advent of railways. From Liverpool came raw cotton and from Hull, Baltic timber, coal and manufactures from Lancashire and Yorkshire, building stone from the Pennines, corn from Lincolnshire and salt from Cheshire – all passed along the canal. Not least,

barges left Manchester laden with stable dung, street sweeping and "nightsoil" to enhance the fertility of the hinterland.

Warehouses, factories and canal arms proliferated around the hub of the Rochdale Canal in Dale Street, and around the adjoining basin of the Ashton Canal, itself from 1811 part of a trans-Pennine link via the Huddersfield Canal. Much of this has now disappeared, but one testament to the prosperity and confidence of the Rochdale Canal Company survives: "a gateway built of stone rusticated" which the committee ordered in 1822 be erected at the entrance to the Manchester wharves.

2. IRWELL, IRK AND MEDLOCK

Manchester city centre is bounded to the west by the river Irwell, which forms part of the boundary with Salford, and to the north and south respectively by the rather less noticeable Rivers Irk and Medlock. Lesser streams, such as the River Tib and Shooters Brook, are now entirely culverted (see G. Ashworth: The Lost Rivers of Manchester, 1987).

The Irk and the Medlock degenerated rapidly in the early industrial revolution. Writers such as Dr James Kay (in 1832) and Frederick Engels (in 1844) describe coal-black foul streams, fed by the outfall from sewers, dye works, gas works, bone works and tanneries, checked every few yards by high factory weirs, behind which accumulated slime and rotting refuse.

Some of the worst of the working class housing was to be found alongside the Irk and the Medlock. In "Little Ireland" on the Medlock near Oxford Road two hundred inhabitations were crowded together, frequently flooded. This district, wrote Kay, had been the haunt of thieves and desperadoes, and "was

always inhabited by a class resembling savages in their appetites and habits." On the south bank of the Irk (at a spot now underneath Victoria Station), families were crammed into cottages around courts which also contained pig styes and catgut and tripe manufactories. Across the river was a tannery, four storeys high and filled with skins, and the parish burial ground, "chiefly used as a place of interment for paupers."

The Irwell, with a greater volume of water and less obstructions, was usually less horrific. Barges came up the Mersey and Irwell Navigation (opened around 1734) to quays around Quay Street. By the 19th century, some barges were being poled up the river as far as Hunts Bank, bringing timber to a yard on the site of the later Exchange Station. On the Manchester side of the river, at a landing stage just below Victoria Bridge, rowing boats were for hire, and small steamers started for pleasure trips down the river to Pomona Gardens "and other holiday resorts" (J. Corbett: The River Irwell. 1907).

3. CASTLEFIELD

The Roman fort of Mamucium was built at Castlefield (hence the name), on a bank above the Medlock, close to the confluence with the Irwell, in AD 79. Below the site of the fort, 1,686 years later, the Duke of Bridgewater established the terminus of what can be described as England's first canal. Roman remains, canal, wharves and warehouses, together with the world's first passenger railway station, are now part of Britain's first Urban Heritage Park, so designated in 1982.

The Bridgewater Canal, which was soon connected to the Mersey at Runcorn and to canals leading to the midlands and the east, was originally conceived as a means of supplying coal from the Duke's mines at Worsley to the fast growing market in Manchester and Salford. "On the execution of the undertaking, the poor in those towns were benefited by a reduction in the price of coals of one half of what they before paid," wrote Dr John Aikin, "and vast quantities were taken away by them from the wharf in Castlefield, in wheelbarrows, at three-pence halfpenny per hundred" (*A Description of the Country 30-40 Miles Around Manchester*, 1795).

The Castlefield site had the advantage that the River Medlock could be used to feed the canal; but it lay at the bottom of a steep and difficult sandstone bank. The solution of the Duke and his engineer James Brindley to this problem was described by a German observer, Johann Hogrewe: "A canal cut through the rock leads underneath Castlefield, and almost at the end of it there is a round shaft which opens out above into the open air. A crane was standing over it, which, when set in motion by a waterwheel, hauled up the coal in crates of 800 pounds which are guided under this shaft. The advantage was that coal could now be transported to the town on a level road ..." (quoted in LD Bradshaw: *Visitors to Manchester*, 1987). The Grocers Warehouse, later built across the entrance to the tunnel, and also using a water-powered hoist, has been partially reconstructed.

LE

the Castlefield Canal Basin

New Mills to Mellor

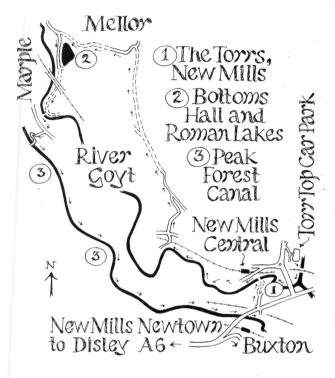

Mellor

Marple

② Bottoms

River Goyt

③

N↑

① The Torrs, New Mills

② Bottoms Hall and Roman Lakes

③ Peak Forest Canal

New Mills Central

Torr Top Car Park

①

New Mills Newtown to Disley A6 ← Buxton

LENGTH OF WALK: Approximately 8 miles.

DEGREE OF DIFFICULTY: Low.

PUBLIC TRANSPORT: New Mills has two railway stations. New Mills Central is on the line from Manchester, Romiley and Marple to Sheffield via the Hope Valley; New Mills Newtown is on the line from Manchester, Stockport, Hazel Grove and Disley to Whaley Bridge, Chapel-en-le-Frith, and Buxton. New Mills bus station is served by buses from Macclesfield (via Rainow), Buxton, Chapel, Whaley Bridge, Marple, Hazel Grove, Glossop and Stockport.

ORDNANCE SURVEY MAP: At 1:25,000, this walk can be found on Outdoor Leisure Map 1: The Peak District – Dark Peak Area. Alternatively, all but a few yards at the eastern end of the walk can be found on Pathfinder Map 741: Stockport (South).

This walk begins in the truly spectacular but hidden and under-appreciated gorge of the Torrs Riverside Park in the industrial

revolution cotton town of New Mills. We leave the Torrs by the
elegant new Millennium Walkway, suspended above the rocky
torrent of the River Goyt, emerging in the fields of the wider
valley downstream. At Hague Bar we climb the valley side by
narrow lanes. We pass through Brook Bottom, said to be the
smallest village in Derbyshire, and follow lanes and tracks
along the hillside toward Mellor, before dropping down an old
quarry track into the valley of the Goyt, narrow and wooded
once more. Here, Bottoms Hall and Farm mark the site of
Samuel Oldknow's attempt to establish a rural industrial
community early in the industrial revolution. We now head back
upstream, passing the Roman lakes and crossing the Roman
bridge to the Cheshire side of the Goyt, before climbing up to the
towpath of the Peak Forest Canal, along which we return to
New Mills, enjoying the excellent views across the valley to
Mellor, Cobden Edge, and, eventually, to Kinder Scout in the
distance with, perhaps, the Kinder Downfall glinting in the
sunlight.

The best access to the starting point of this walk, the **Torrs
Gorge (1)** in central New Mills, is down the narrow cobbled
track by derelict weavers' cottages at the side of Torr Top car
park, Torr Top Street. Bear right, and walk under the arch of
the railway viaduct down to the River Sett, and on to the
confluence with the River Goyt. Here, by a mighty weir, are the
remains of Torr Mill. Bear right, following the Goyt
downstream through the canyon. Pass under the viaduct which
takes Union Road across the gorge. On the right a path leads
up to the New Mills Heritage Centre and to the bus station; we
continue by the river past the remains of Rock Mill and across
the Millennium Walkway. Torr Vale Mill stands opposite, grand
but grim.

The riverside path leads to the quiet road which has come
down into the valley past New Mills Central Station. Continue
ahead along the road for a few yards, then follow the "Goyt
Way" marked path on the right across the now-reclaimed site of
the former gasworks. A track is joined; turn right, walk past a
ruined barn, and beyond take the GW marked path to the left.
After passing through the trees planted on the site of a former
tip, at a track by the river, take the riverside path downstream.
Walk for about a third of a mile by the river through the fields,
then go up the bank by steps on the right, which lead up to
Hague Bar car park, picnic site and playground.

Cross the bridge over the railway and walk up to the main
road. Cross straight over into Hague Fold Road, which climbs
rather steeply up the hillside. Follow the road as it twists left
in front of Higher Hague Fold Farm, becoming a track. At the
tarmac road ahead turn left. Here, we get a good view of two
old industrial sites in the Goyt valley below: Disley paper mill,
and, downstream, the former printworks site at Strines
(operating by 1792).

Continue along the narrow quiet lane to the tiny village of Brook Bottom. In front of the Fox Inn the Goyt Way follows a track on the left, but we continue past the pub, following the road to the right, then turn left, climbing out of Brook Bottom past the former Primitive Methodist chapel. After about half a mile on this road/track, opposite "The Cottage", take the track on the right, and follow this straight ahead for about a mile. The track climbs gently, and then, passing an ostrich farm on the left, descends equally gently across the Mellor and Towncliffe golf course.

Just before the track becomes a proper road, on the far side of the golf course near the hamlet of Tarden, turn left, then immediately left again on the tarred track which is signed as leading to the main golf club car park. After a few yards this road twists right, and we now follow the route of an old straight track from the former Cobden Quarry down into the valley. Beyond the cross tracks, a stretch of old flagged pathway can still be seen. Above the "Roman Lakes", the track twists right, descending to **Bottoms Hall (2)**.

Samuel Oldknow's large cotton mill of 1793 was sited a few hundred yards further on, but we turn left just below Bottoms Hall, into Lakes Road. This track follows the mill leat back to the mill pool, or lakes, and then follows the Goyt upstream, under the railway viaduct, and past a hexagonal cottage built by Oldknow as a toll house.

A few hundred yards further on, take the path on the right which leads to the "Roman" bridge, which is actually a packhorse bridge of the 18th century, originally known as Windybottom Bridge. Over the bridge, follow the path to the left by the river. Pass between two cottages, and walk up their driveway to Strines Road. Cross, and walk up Plucksbridge Road until you reach the **Peak Forest Canal (3)**, and turn left onto the towpath.

Our route now follows the towpath as the canal winds through fields and woods (mostly) for three miles to New Mills Newtown. Look out for a railway below the canal on the left: this is the Midland main line from Manchester, opened in 1902, which has just emerged into the valley from Disley tunnel. Nearer to Newtown, you may become aware of another railway, the Stockport to Buxton line, opened in 1857, above the canal on the right. The valley is thus occupied here by three railways, in addition to the canal and the A6 road, the noise from which accompanies us into Newtown.

Five steam powered cotton mills were built next to the canal at Newtown between 1850 and 1872. We pass between Brunswick Mill (on the left) and Albion Mill (on the right). Immediately beyond, bridge 28 takes the A6015 Hayfield road across the canal. Pass under the bridge, walk on for a few yards, then turn left following a path to a side road, and walk down to the main road.

Cross straight over and walk down Wirksmoor Road. Where

Millennium Walk, New Mills

Most of the weight of the bridge was taken on a floating caisson, which can be seen under the bridge. This and the similar Town Bridge downstream (opened 1899) were the first in Britain to be operated by electricity.

Walk along the riverside path. Before the Town Bridge, cross the open ground to the left, and turn left on Castle Street. The car showroom on the right occupies the site of the much-photographed subsidence of Castle Chambers in 1891.

Turn right into Verdin Park, and follow the park roadway which climbs up the hill. At the top end of the park are railway sidings on the branch line leading to the chemical works at Winnington. Cross the railway by the footbridge. Follow the road beyond between houses and parkland, and continue straight ahead to a busier road. Turn right and walk up to the traffic lights. Cross the main road, then turn right into Solvay Road. The houses here were built by **Brunner Mond (2)** in the 1870s and 1880s. The street names commemorate pioneers of the chemical industry.

Walk to the bottom of Solvay Road and turn left into Park Road. On the right are the sports field and pavilion (which contained baths, reading room, concert hall, library and billiard tables) opened by Brunner Mond in 1901.

Turn right into Runcorn Road, and walk past the Winnington Works (on the right) and then past the Wallerscote Works (on the left) where ICI opened the world's first commercial polythene plant in 1938. Carry on along Runcorn Road, across the Weaver, and then across the Navigation cut by Winnington swing bridge. At the T-junction beyond the swing bridge carry straight on by using the path which leads up through Bestway Wood to the Trent and Mersey Canal (fully opened 1777).

Turn right onto the towpath. Our walk now follows the towpath for about two and a half miles to the Lion Salt Works at Marston. The most obvious feature passed on the way (after half a mile) is the Anderton Boat Lift, opened in 1875 to provide a connection between the canal and the river navigation below. The lift closed in 1982, but the Anderton Boat Lift Trust is working to raise funds to restore and manage it.

A little under a mile from the boat lift, after the canal has swung around the contours and crossed the Marbury Brook, brine pipes cross the canal. High brick walls beyond enclose the site of Marbury Pumping Station, where from 1882 steam engines forced brine along a pipeline to Weston Point near Runcorn, hastening the decline of the Northwich salt making industry.

Many salt works and rock salt mines occupied canalside sites from this point. Subsidence caused a canal burst in 1907 where the canal crosses Forge Brook (opposite the point where Marbury Park woods on the left end). The straight concrete lined stretch of canal beyond was opened in 1958, to avoid subsidence on the original line, which lay to the right.

The next bridge is Ollershaw Lane Bridge. Leave the towpath here and turn right down Ollershaw Lane. Access to the **Lion Salt Works (3)** is via the former Lion Inn. Our route continues along

Ollershaw Lane, and then straight on along New Warrington Road. To the right, subsidence led to the formation of broad lakes known as Ashton's and Neumann's Flashes. From 1938 to the 1950s ICI piped lime waste, a useless by-product of soda ash manufacture, into the Flashes. The retaining walls were grassed over, and coarse vegetation now covers the solidified lagoons.

It is necessary now to walk for about a third of a mile on the footpath by this sometimes busy road, after which cross the footbridge on the left over the brook. A rather overgrown path climbs the riverbank to the left. Note upstream the bridge of the old branch railway to the salt works. Climb the stile at the top of the bank, and cross the field to another stile which can be seen ahead. Beyond is a track: follow this to the main road. Turn right, then cross over. Northwich railway station lies beyond the Tesco store.

1. HUNT'S LOCKS

The River Weaver runs through the central Cheshire saltfields from Nantwich through Winsford and Northwich to the Mersey estuary at Frodsham. The river was useless for transport until it was converted (as far up as Winsford) to a toll-charging Navigation, which opened in 1732. Salt for export and for the coasting trade could now be sent more cheaply down the river to the Mersey, and coal from the south Lancashire coalfield could be brought up-river to the brine boilers.

The Weaver Navigation initially had eleven small wooden locks. But as the salt trade grew through the 18th and 19th centuries the river was repeatedly improved by the construction of longer embanked cuts and fewer, bigger, locks. After the final rebuilding, between 1874 and 1897, only four pairs of locks remained: Hunt's Locks, Vale Royal Locks between Northwich and Winsford, and

the bridge at Hunt's Lock

rightwards direction, but to look at Lyme Hall and its immediate surroundings, turn left onto the road, and walk down into the hollow. (**3. Lyme Hall**).

Return along the tarred road. Over the rise, bear left along the road. Continue through the gate and along the track which leads down through a wooded valley to West Lodge at the boundary of the park. Turn right onto the track which passes in front of the lodge. At the top of the hill follow the track as it bears left, and walk along it to Green Farm (the Lyme Park boundary wall is over to your right all the way). Bear left in front of the farm buildings, and a few yards further on follow the track round to the left. As the track descends the hillside, good views of the lowlands open up. Just before Throstlenest Farm, take the field path on the left. This swings to the right and descends the hill, by-passing the farm. Continue downhill below the farm – ignore the stile in the hedge on the right. Walk on down to a footbridge over the canal (bridge 16). Traces of an adjacent swingbridge can still be seen.

Cross the bridge and turn right, following the hawthorn-shaded path which runs parallel to the canal towpath for a few feet, and then swings left. Walk down the track, which passes by Hagg Farm. Just before the track swings to the left, take the path on the right which leads down to Poynton Brook. Cross the footbridge, and follow the path on boardwalks down the marshy wooded valley. At the end of the causeway, climb up the steps on the right. The path opens onto a driveway, with the road a little further on. Turn left onto the road, then right onto the Middlewood Way. Cross straight over the former railway and take the path next to the Poynton Coppice information board. There are many paths in the coppice: keep to the top of the valley, on the edge of the woods. Beyond a gateway, turn right and join a tarred track which passes between kennels on the right and a covered reservoir on the left. Follow the main track, bearing right then left, to Coppice Road.

Slightly to the left across the road is a signed path leading between houses to the fields behind. Bear left across the first field, walking more or less parallel to, but some yards away from, the gardens of the roadside houses. The path is not clear, but there is a stile in the fence ahead. Go through, and walk with the fence on your left to another stile. In the field beyond, the path is again difficult to detect. Walk across in line with the previous path, and you will come to a stile in another fence. Continue ahead, crossing the field diagonally. Over a rise, a few isolated trees can be seen in the field. A colliery tramway once ran across the field below these, but it is difficult now to detect any trace. Another tramway ran alongside the belt of trees on the right. Make for the stile at the edge of the woods in the field corner ahead.

A short track leads down to the junction of Anson Road and Middlewood Road. Turn left down Middlewood Road. The route back to the centre of Poynton lies along roads which can be fairly busy, but you pass some of the buildings of the early industrial community. Petre Bank, a long row of whitewashed cottages dated 1815, can be seen on the right. After a hundred yards or so, stonework on either side of the road marks the site of a tramway bridge, on the skew. Round the curve, on the right, is the site of Lady Pit – where a brick engine house survives. Middlewood Road now meets Coppice Road to form Park Lane. Carry straight on. After about a third of a mile, on the left, set back from the road, is Long Row, built by Lord Vernon in 1844. A little further down the road, on the right, is the Poynton Centre, formerly the Vernon Schools.

Continue along Park Lane to return to the car park, or to the bus stops or the railway station.

1. POYNTON TRAMWAYS AND MINES

Coal was being mined in Poynton by the 16th century but the rapid growth of large scale mining came with the industrial revolution from the late 18th century. The opening of the Macclesfield Canal in 1831 and the railways in 1845 and 1869 encouraged further development, including the extension of the colliery tramways into a complex network. Bagshaw's trade directory of 1850 noted that "the Poynton and Worth coal mines, the property of (and worked by) the Right Hon. George Warren, Lord Vernon, are numerous, and spread over a compass of two miles. The coal is of good quality, and the mines are very prolific, having seams of coal varying from 2 feet to 7 feet in thickness."

The Vernon family were paternalistic, as Morris's 1874 directory indicates: "His Lordship supports some excellent schools on the national system, for the purpose of educating the children of the colliers and poor ... the Poynton Library and Newsroom, established in 1854 by his Lordship for the benefit of his workmen, contains upward of three hundred volumes ... there are six neat almshouses in the gothic style which have been erected by Lord Vernon for the aged and infirm workpeople, who have an allowance of 2s 6d per week, and coals."

The mines of the area had employed over a thousand men and boys in the middle of the 19th century. The number had fallen to 250 by 1935, when the last pit closed. Most of the tramway rails were taken up in the following year.

2. THE MACCLESFIELD CANAL

The Macclesfield Canal runs along the edge of the east Cheshire hills from Kidsgrove in the south to Marple in the north. The canal provided the local community with cheaper transport for coal, stone and foodstuffs, but it also formed a link in the national waterway system – previously, boats bound for the midlands and the south from Manchester and the industrial area to its east had to go almost as far as Runcorn on the Bridgewater Canal, before turning south on the Trent and Mersey. The need for the Macclesfield Canal had long been obvious, but previous attempts had been opposed by the Bridgewater interests. When an Act was finally obtained, in 1826, the canal age was almost finished. In the previous year the Stockton to Darlington railway had opened and the Liverpool and Manchester railway was authorised. A few far-sighted individuals

argued for an east Cheshire railway instead of a canal – but the rural gentry did not relish the prospect of "smoking steam carriages" being visible from their estates. The Macclesfield Canal had a short life as a mainstream element in the national transport system; as a consequence its finely engineered bridges, stonework and locks show relatively little wear and tear.

3. LYME HALL AND PARK

Lyme Hall is surrounded by 1,400 acres of parkland, some of it open moor. The herd of red deer may be descended from the deer of the medieval Macclesfield Forest, out of which the park was created. The park was also home to a herd of huge and ferocious white cattle, greatly feared by the locals and a deterrent to poachers. You won't meet any on this walk: the last remnant of the herd was destroyed in 1884.

Lyme Hall is an amalgamation of buildings dating from the 16th to the 19th centuries. The famous south front overlooking the lake was built by Giacomo Leoni in 1720. The Legh family lived at Lyme from its foundation in the 14th century up to the 20th century. Their wealth was much increased during the industrial revolution as they possessed estates on the Lancashire coalfield around Newton le Willows. The family was ennobled in 1892, and spent its wealth conspicuously at Lyme.

Sumptuous and extended celebrations were mounted for the silver wedding of Lord and Lady Newton in 1905, for the coming of age of their son in 1910, and his wedding in 1914. Heavier taxation and declining income ended this sort of display; after the Second World War, the third baron Newton gave the hall and park to the National Trust. **LE**

Bridge 15, Macclesfield Canal

Lyme Park in Winter

Prestbury to Mottram

N

LENGTH OF WALK: Approx. 4.5 miles.

DEGREE OF DIFFICULTY: Easy

PUBLIC TRANSPORT: Prestbury is on the Manchester-Macclesfield railway line, and is served by buses from Macclesfield and Wilmslow.

ORDNANCE SURVEY MAP: At 1:25000 this walk can be found on Pathfinder Map 759 (Macclesfield and Alderley Edge).

From the bridge over the Bollin in Prestbury (where the river is paved, though not with gold as you might expect) the route of this walk passes terraced cottages built during the village's industrial phase in the early 19th century, and the site of Prestbury silk mill. We are soon out in the fields, passing what may have been a medieval leper hospital. Field paths through rolling countryside take us to Mottram St. Andrew, passing 17th century Lee Hall, medieval Mottram Old Hall, and 18th century Mottram Hall, now buzzing with activity as a hotel and conference centre. Public footpaths cross the golf courses at the front and back of the hotel. We walk through woodland to the Bollin, which is crossed on a high footbridge, and return to Prestbury along the quiet riverside path.

From a starting point near the centre of the village of Prestbury, this walk follows field paths and tracks through rolling countryside to Mottram Hall, and returns by a path along the bank of the River Bollin.

In Prestbury, parking is available on Springfields, off New Road, to the east of the bridge over the Bollin.

Walk to the bridge, and turn into Bollin Grove, a straight road which runs parallel to the river for some yards, then on past former workers' cottages and the site of a former **Silk Mill (1)**, near the present Tennis Club.

Continue ahead where the road becomes a track, passing through fields. Follow the track across a bridge over the Bollin, and up toward Spittle House, which is possibly the site of a medieval leper hospital. Just before the entrance to the grounds, take the field path on the left, which follows the Spittle House grounds boundary around to the right. Waymarks show the way.

You will encounter a stile on the right. Cross over the stile and follow the path down into a small valley, crossing a stream by a wooden walkway. The path swings to the left, and then climbs the bank, before emerging into a field.

Follow the fence which is on your left to the end of the field, then turn left, and walk with the fence and a pond to your right. This is the site of the former Lower Gadhole Farm. Go through the stile next to a gate on your right, then follow the gravelled track round to the left, climbing up below Woodend Farm (formerly Upper Gadhole Farm).

The track emerges onto a tarmac drive. Cross over and take the field path, where a finger post shows that this is the way to Mottram St Andrew. Walk ahead across the fields. A wooden walkway crosses a boggy patch in a dip beside an old sycamore. Waymarks show the path up the other side, and at the top of the rise.

Cross the fields, keeping the hedge to your left. Continue ahead up a hill; at the top follow the hedge around to the right, as far as a wooden fingerpost indicating the way to Wilmslow. Go through the iron kissing gate, and walk ahead along a cobbled driveway, and through a waymarked gate. To the right, set back, can be seen the mellow stone facade of Lee Hall.

Immediately beyond, turn right, passing between the hall and a 19th century brick building, then walk straight on through another kissing gate, and across the field. In the second field, keep the hedge and trees to your left as you walk down the gentle slope. Before a wooden fence, cross a stile on the left, and walk diagonally down the field toward a metal farm gate.

Walk through the yard. Beyond the outbuildings, turn left, then immediately right (at a fingerpost) along a track. Before you reach farm buildings, take the path on the left which crosses the Mottram Hall golf course. Continue straight ahead, passing into a field between woods. Walk down to the tree lined drive which leads to Mottram Hall. The black and white Mottram Old Hall can be glimpsed through the trees on the left.

Mottram Hall (2) is now a hotel, and the drive is often busy. Cross the drive with care, and walk across the golf course, making for the far end of the hotel extension (the path is waymarked).

Turn right, and pass between the hotel and the Golf Centre clubhouse. Continue ahead, along a roadway with a car park on the left. Beyond skips at the end of the road, a path leads into trees. After a few feet, cross directly over a track, and follow the path which runs beneath trees.

Again, we emerge onto the golf course. Carry straight on, making for the finger post which is visible on the other side, against the trees. Here, follow the path to the right. Trees, and the steep bank of the Bollin, are on your left. After another set of finger posts, our path swings left down to a footbridge over the river.

Cross the bridge, turn right and follow the path beside the **River Bollin (3)** back to Prestbury. Note the banks of glacial sands, and the multi-coloured pebbles in the river bed, consisting of stones brought from the Irish Sea and the Lake District by the Devensian ice sheet.

For part of the way, the path passes between the river and the sewage treatment works. This stretch is much more pleasant and interesting than it sounds – the vegetation is lush, and the wildlife abundant; you may see a kingfisher here.

The riverside path joins the track which leads to Bollin Grove, our starting point.

1. PRESTBURY SILK MILL SITE

For nearly a century, a textile mill stood on land known as "the Eyes" near the site of the present Prestbury Tennis Club. Peter Downes of Butley Hall in 1790 leased land here to Samuel, William, Joseph and James Reddish, cotton manufacturers of Prestbury, with permission to erect a factory, and use the water of the Bollin to move the machinery.

The lease mentioned that the eastern side of the plot was bounded by "a certain road or way called the Mill Lane". This must have taken its name from the old Butley corn mill, which was presumably situated somewhere downstream.

Many of the small water powered cotton mills put up in the early years of the industrial revolution were converted to other uses from the 1820s. The mill erected by the Reddishes was taken over for silk throwing by Joseph Swanwick in 1825, and seems to have been operated as a silk mill up to the 1870s.

Nothing of the mill now survives, but we can still see the adjacent row of workers' cottages (originally fifteen) which seem to have been erected in 1825, presumably by Swanwick. The leat carrying water from the Bollin to the mill pool passed directly in front of the cottages. Catherine Oates, aged two, drowned here in 1845; at the inquest held in the Admiral Rodney "it was mentioned as a matter of surprise that more children as well as grown up people have not lost their lives in this cut, particularly by night, as it is open to the public road and quite unguarded, down to the factory, a distance of 200 yards."

2. MOTTRAM HALL

Mottram Old Hall was erected in the late middle ages as a semi-fortified manor house, and was extended in the early 17th century. It survived the building of a new hall in the 1750s because it was put to use as the Mottram estate agent's house.

The new hall was built by William Wright of Offerton Hall near Stockport, who had bought the Mottram estate in 1738. There appear to be no surviving family papers or contemporary accounts to tell us about the circumstances of the building of the new hall. "Much too little known" says Pevsner, referring either to the hall itself or to its history.

The original buildings, to the south of the recent hotel extensions, consist of a pedimented and pilastered centre, parallel wings on each side, and further wings extending forward. In addition to the central doorway with a broken pediment there are four more rusticated doorways in the frontage. "What were they needed for?" asks Pevsner.

Wright had built the hall for his son, Randal, who died aged 21 in 1753. His six other children had died before they reached the age of 20. Wright erected a huge monument to his children in St Mary's church, Stockport, and built there a new church, St Peter's.

For these facts, I am indebted to de Figuereido and Treuherz's *Cheshire Country Houses* (1988). As the authors imply, it is unsurprising that William Wright's own memorial in St Peter's records "a life of 73 years, embittered with pain and trouble".

Mottram Hall

3. THE RIVER BOLLIN

The Bollin, which rises in the east Cheshire hills, has been prone to rise suddenly during storms: the name Bollin may be partly derived from "hylnn", meaning a rushing torrent.

One of the worst floods in the 19th century occurred on a June night in 1872. The local paper reported that it was "difficult to recognise as the Bollin the large volume of water which rushed through Prestbury overflowing its bank for 50 or 60 yards on either side, spreading devastation and destruction in its course." The corn mill bridge was washed away; beer barrels in the cellar of the Admiral Rodney were "turned topsy turvy"; a sick woman had to be rescued by boat from the upstairs window of a cottage; pigs and poultry floated down the swollen river towards Wilmslow.

For the residents of Prestbury, however, floods had the advantage that they scoured away the industrial pollution and sewage which came down the river from Macclesfield and tended to settle on the riverbed when the water was low.

In 1865, a very dry summer coincided with rumours of plans by the Macclesfield Board of Health to construct new sewers "with a view to turning the whole sewage of that town into the River Bollin". In Prestbury, an emergency vestry meeting was called, and many of the inhabitants stood up to describe the effects of "Macclesfield delight" in the river.

Dr Frank Renaud, an early commuter, stated that "frequently on leaving the smoky suburbs of Manchester he had reached his home in Prestbury in the hope of enjoying the pure atmosphere of a rural village, but only to experience a stench so intolerable that often, if he could, he would have gone back to the foul air of Manchester..."

It is not so strange therefore that many of the residents of Prestbury were not averse to the eventual construction, in 1896, of a main drainage scheme in Macclesfield, with a sewage farm at Butley, downstream of Prestbury village. **LE**

River Bollin at Prestbury

104

The Roaches to Tittesworth Reservoir

Alternative Routes

① Tittesworth Reservoir
② The Roaches
③ The Mills of Upper Hulme

Roche Grange

Roach Side Farm

N

Frith Bottom

Hen Cloud

Meerbrook

Whitly Lane

Car Park and Visitor Centre

①

LENGTH OF WALK: Approximately nine miles.

DEGREE OF DIFFICULTY: Medium

PUBLIC TRANSPORT: On summer weekends, a bus service links Leek with the Tittesworth Reservoir Amenity Area and car park near Meerbrook, where this walk begins.

ORDNANCE SURVEY MAP: At 1:25,000, this walk can be found on Outdoor Leisure map 24: The Peak District, White Peak Area.

This walk begins at the north end of Tittesworth Reservoir, near the Staffordshire village of Meerbrook, and gives access to visually dramatic countryside which is rich in medieval associations. We follow field paths up the valley north of Meerbrook, between Gun Hill and the Roaches, which was cleared of its natural oak and alder woodland by the Cistercian monks of nearby Dieulacres Abbey in the 13th century. We gradually climb to the rocky spine of the Roaches, to survey the area which may have been the setting of the

*climax of the 14th century alliterative poem, Gawain and the Green
Knight. After walking the length of the Roaches, we descend a
narrow rocky wooded valley behind Hen Cloud, past the remains of
an ancient water mill, and emerge at the industrial hamlet of Upper
Hulme. We return to Meerbrook beside the old abandoned Leek-
Buxton road, part of which is now a deep muddy tree-shaded
holloway.*

Whether you arrive by bus or by car, **Tittesworth Reservoir (1)**
car park makes a useful starting point for this walk. If you come by
car, you will need to follow signs for Meerbrook from the A53 Leek-
Buxton road, or from the old Leek-Macclesfield road south of
Rushton Spencer.

From the car park, turn left and walk up the road to Meerbrook
village. Turn right at the Lazy Trout. After a few hundred yards on
a quiet lane, take the waymarked path on the right and follow a
grassed-over track to the ruined Lower Lee Farm. Beyond, follow
the field path to the left. At a track, carry straight on, with the
hedge on your right. After two stiles, the path turns right and goes
round the edge of a field. Look out for a bridge across a stream on
the right. Cross, and walk straight on across two fields, after which
the lane from Meerbrook is encountered again. Turn right onto the
lane, which immediately swings sharply to the left.

You may wish to follow the road for about three quarters of a
mile, up to another very sharp bend (to the right), and from there
carry straight on along a track. Our map however shows the route
described below, which is a little longer but avoids quite so much
road-walking.

Just around the sharp left-hand bend, take the field path on the
right, and follow this straight ahead through three fields to Roach
Side Farm. The path passes behind the house through a
waymarked gateway on the right. Once clear of the house, climb the
stile to the left and follow field paths to the road. Walk ahead for
about a quarter of a mile, until the road swings sharp right just
before the farms and houses of Roche Grange. At this point begin to
walk along the track ahead, but after the cattle grid turn left into
the field. No path is visible here, but the right of way shown on the
OS map swings round to the right below the crest of the rise which
is to your right, then runs diagonally down the field to join a track
below beyond a ragged line of trees. Turn right along the track, and
walk ahead up the valley, ignoring a path to the left.

Beyond a ladder stile, continue up the valley for some yards
before crossing a bridge over the stream. Bear right after the
bridge, walking above the stream, then bear left toward the top of
the hill. Go through the gate, and cross the field to Buxton Brow
Farm. Turn right on the track, and walk up through the farm
buildings to the narrow lane beyond. Turn right and walk up the
lane until it ends beyond Clough Head Farm. Take the concrete
track on the left, and follow it for about half a mile to the point
where it swings left to descend to a farm. Here, carry straight on
across a field to a point where paths cross.

Take the path to the right, which leads along the ridge back toward the Roaches. Cross a narrow lane and continue ahead on the well-used and partly paved path which runs along the top of the **Roaches (2)**. The dip-slope of the Roaches on the left leads down to the synclinal basin of Goldsitch Moss, where coal was mined in a small way in the 18th and 19th centuries and perhaps earlier.

Continue along the top of the Roaches, through dissected and weirdly weathered rocks and on past Doxey Pool. As the path descends, a wall appears on the right. Walk to the end of this, and then turn right into the gully beyond. Rough steps lead down into pinewoods. At the bottom, follow the path around to the left, and walk along below the climbers' rock faces. Eventually, in front of pinnacles of rock, steps lead down to the right then round to the left. Ahead is Rockhall, a former gamekeeper's lodge, now used as a climbers' refuge. Walk down to the gateway in the wall below Rockhall and turn left, passing in front of its enclosure, and walk down to a stone surfaced track.

Turn left and walk along the track as far as the second stile on the right. Cross the stile, walk directly across the field, and turn sharp left after the stile on the other side. A rough path leads down to a field next to Well Farm. A waymarker shows the way: bear right and then left, joining the farm track below the farm.

Walk down the track for about a quarter of a mile. Where the track swings sharply to the right, carry straight on across the grass for a few yards, then cross a stile on the right, and walk ahead, bearing left and then right, around a knoll. Our route now follows Back Brook down its narrow valley to the **Mills of Upper Hulme (3)**. The presence of springs ensures that there are persistent patches of mud. One of these, crossed by a wooden walkway, is at the site of the small millpool above Dains Mill; the mill ruins lie just below. Beyond the mill we join a track which leads down to the village of Upper Hulme.

At the village, follow the road straight on, across the ford and bridge, between factory buildings. The road swings to the right and climbs up through a narrow shady gap: be very careful here, as visibility for the Roaches traffic which uses this lane may be poor. Toward the top of this steep stretch, take the second farm-type entrance on the left: a concrete roadway leading down to a metal farm gate. Go through this gate and the next, bearing right around farm buildings, and emerging on a track. After a few yards, a finger post shows the path on the left which leads down to a second finger post. Turn right here, in the direction of Meerbrook.

A line of trees marks the line of Whitty Lane, part of the ancient route from Leek to Buxton, now a holloway occupied for part of its length by a stream. The path lies in the field, with the old lane to the left, for a few hundred yards. Look out for a stile on the left, beyond which steps lead down into the hollow, where the stream is crossed on stone slabs. On the other side, the route lies directly across a field to the track which is visible ahead. Walk along the track to the road and turn right.

This road leads direct to our starting point, a distance of about a third of a mile. There is no roadside footpath, and the first stretch has little in the way of verges. Traffic for Tittesworth Reservoir can be quite heavy, especially at weekends. If you wish to avoid most of this road and return to Meerbrook by field paths, go through the stile which you will see on the right after a few yards. The route is shown on our map; it is part of the "Staffordshire Moorlands Walk" and is waymarked as such. If you follow this path, an extra two miles or so will be added to the walk.

1. TITTESWORTH RESERVOIR

Tittesworth Reservoir, though originally much smaller, today extends for nearly a mile and a half through the valley of the River Churnet, up to the edge of the village of Meerbrook. In the early middle ages, this was thickly wooded land, as many surviving local place names testify. The Old English "frith" means woodland. Frith Bottom is at the northern end of the reservoir; Meerbrook lay within the township of Leekfrith. "Lea", "lee", or "leigh" can mean woodland, or a woodland clearing. A glance at the two and a half inch OS map will show a cluster of place names containing this element to the north and east of Meerbrook.

The fairly rapid clearance of much of the woodland (which has been confirmed by analysis of pollen preserved in local peat) took place after the establishment of the Cistercian Abbey of Dieulacres in the Churnet Valley just north of Leek, in 1214. The abbey was endowed with the old manor of Rudyard, the boundary of which seems to have run through Meerbrook ("Meer" means boundary), and the monks soon acquired more land, including that to the north of Meerbrook. Cistercians vowed to cultivate the wilderness; their sheep farms (known as granges, and run by lay brethren) produced wool commercially, on a large scale. Roach Grange below the

Tittesworth Reservoir

108

Roaches, had been established in 1246; New Grange, to the south-east of Meerbrook village, by 1291.

The first Tittesworth Reservoir was about half the size of the present one. It was opened in 1858 by the Staffordshire Potteries Water Works Company as a compensation reservoir, to ensure a regular supply of water to mills along the Churnet which would be affected by the company's use of springs in the valley. The raising of the dam and extension of the reservoir took place between 1959 and 1962. New Grange Farm, and a former corn mill site near Meerbrook were drowned, and the road up from Leek past the old Abbey site to Meerbrook was diverted on the west side of the reservoir. Water from the reservoir is now cleaned in treatment works below the dam, before being supplied to Severn Trent customers in Leek and Stoke.

2. THE ROACHES

The broken, tumbled and weathered rocks on the escarpment of the high gritstone outcrop known as the Roaches (meaning simply

Rockhall cottage

"rocks") bear testimony of an erosional regime much more severe than today's. The results are perfectly described in the north-west midlands Middle English of the late fourteenth century poem *Gawain and the Green Knight*: "rughe knockled knarres with korned stones". Professor Ralph Elliott identified this countryside as that in which Sir Gawain searched for the Green Knight, and believed the "Green Chapel" of the poem to be Lud's Church, a natural chasm a mile or so north-west of the Roaches (North Staffordshire Journal of Field Studies, 1977). It is tempting to imagine that the "Gawain poet" might have been a monk of Dieulacres Abbey. However, many other locations for the poem have been suggested. For instance, Dr J Phillip Dodd, who lived in Frodsham, set the action on the mid-Cheshire ridge (Cheshire History, Autumn 1990).

Up to the 19th century, the Roaches were mostly common wasteland. After enclosure under an Act of 1805 the land became part of the Swythamley estate, which was bought in 1831 by a Macclesfield banker, William Brocklehurst. William's successor as "squire" of Swythamley, Philip Brocklehurst, had the path along the summit of the Roaches constructed in 1860 – for his own use and his visitors', not for the general public.

At the southern end of the Roaches, a cave had served as a dwelling since at least the early 17th century; by 1770 it was known as Rockhall. Its last occupant, Bess Bowyer, who was said to be a descendant of bandits and none too law abiding herself, died in the 1850s. Philip Brocklehurst built the Gothic frontage to the cave and the adjacent cottage in 1861, to serve as a hunting lodge and gamekeeper's house. The Peak Park Board acquired the Roaches in

1980, and Rockhall nine years later. The cottage now serves as a climbers' refuge.

3. THE MILLS OF UPPER HULME

The remote and crumbling Dains Mill is the higher of the two mill sites at Upper Hulme. It has been suggested that the name is derived from springs below an ancient burial mound (Dain Springs – "Springs of the Dead") which fed the mill pool. The truth is likely to be more prosaic: the mill was tenanted in the early 16th century by one Robert Deane. A corn mill had been erected on this site in the late 1560s. It appears to have been demolished after a dispute with the corn mill downstream over the limited supply of water, but to have been rebuilt quickly. It seems to me that the supply of corn as well as water would be limited in these parts, but Dains Mill apparently continued to operate until 1946.

Upper Hulme village, a quarter of a mile downstream, may have been the site of the corn mill granted to Dieulacres Abbey in the early 13th century. Early in the industrial revolution, a water-powered factory was built here: in 1831 it was advertised for lease as a stone-built, four-storey silk mill with "upwards of 300 dozen spindles and other machinery, all new"; in 1869, it was advertised as a flax spinning mill, with dyeing facilities.

The purchaser in 1869 was 32-year-old William Tatton from Leek, who established a silk dyeing business which prospered and grew over the years. William Tatton is described as a Methodist teetotaller, but nonetheless an employer so affectionate toward his workers that he was "not averse to abetting them in minor derelictions of duty, such as ignoring the bell to restart work when he and they had become absorbed in a too-exciting game of marbles."

William Tatton died in 1902, but the growth continued, especially after the Great War, when the firm moved into the preparation of rayon yarn. In 1931 a new mill was built on the site for warping and sizing. In 1970 production was moved to Leek. Today the Upper Hulme buildings house a variety of smaller enterprises. **LE**

Rockhall in the 19th Century

Stockport Town Centre

① Vernon Park
② Market Place
③ Hopes Carr Mills

Bus Station
Shopping Precinct
New Zealand Rd
River Goyt
Town Hall
St Mary's Way
Wood Bank Park
Wellington Road South
Car Park
A 626 to Marple

LENGTH OF WALK: This circular walk in central Stockport is nearly two miles long; the connecting walk from Woodbank Park to Stockport Market Place and back adds a further three miles, approximately.

DEGREE OF DIFFICULTY: Easy.

PUBLIC TRANSPORT: Stockport bus station and railway station are both on the route of the circular town centre walk.

ORDNANCE SURVEY MAP: At 1:25000, the southern part of this walk can be found on Pathfinder map 741 (Stockport South), and the northern part on Pathfinder map 724 (Manchester and Ashton under Lyne). But for this walk, a larger scale A-Z type street map would be more useful.

This walk is essentially a circular town centre walk, which passes both the bus and railway stations of Stockport. But for those who want more exercise, and free parking, a preliminary walk is suggested, starting at Woodbank Park above the southern bank of the River Goyt, passing through the recently restored Vernon Park, and reaching the town at its ancient focus, the Market Place. From here, we drop steeply down toward the site of the bridge over the Mersey -- now culverted -- which provided access from Cheshire into Lancashire. We walk below a sandstone cliff, passing black and white halls on Underbank, and the Air Raid Shelter Museum and Hatting Museum on Chestergate. We climb up past the railway station to Wellington Road, built early in the 19th century as a town by-pass, and walk across to Hillgate, which was the original approach to Stockport from the south. After a detour to look at the

*oldest surviving cotton mill buildings in town we turn, in the
shadow of Robinson's Brewery, into the medievally narrow and
chaotic Little Underbank, before climbing dank steps back up to the
Market Place.*

These directions are written on the assumption that you are going
to walk from Woodbank Park to Stockport Market Place before
completing the circuit of the historic centre of Stockport and then
returning to Woodbank Park.

A large free car park is available at the southern end of
Woodbank Park. Access to the car park is from Turncroft Lane,
which is off the A626 from Marple. Access to Woodbank Park from
the car park is by Park Lane, on the right of the car park as you
enter it.

Woodbank Park, which contains the former residence of one of
Stockport's leading cotton masters, was presented to Stockport
Corporation in 1921 in memory of the Stockport men killed in the
first world war.

Inside the park, having walked down the entrance drive, turn left
in front of the information board. Follow the path past the
childrens' playground to its junction with the spinal park road.
Cross the road and walk over to the path which runs along the edge
of a steep wooded bank above the River Goyt. Follow the path to the
left. Pear Mill (cotton, 1908) can be seen below.

The path leads to a gate in the railings around **Vernon Park
(1)**. The Museum building lies ahead. At this point you can either
take the wooden steps down toward the Goyt, then turn left along
the path near the river, or you can walk toward the museum, then
follow the park path down to the right. Either way, you will end up
in the lower level of Vernon Park.

Leave the park by the low-level exit, beyond the circular pond.
Turn left before the Park Inn, and walk up New Zealand Road
(built in the 1820s largely, it is said, by unemployed men on poor
relief and consequently known as Pinch-Belly Road). As the road
climbs up the bank, there are good views across the industrialised
valley where the Goyt and the Tame join to form the River Mersey.

Near the top of the bank, where New Zealand Road twists to the
left, take the walkway on the right. After a few hundred yards,
cross St Mary's Way, a sort of inner ring road, by the footbridge on
the right. Across the bridge turn left, walk to the end of the houses
and then up the ginnel on the right. You will emerge on an estate
road: follow it ahead and then round to the left, to join Churchgate.
Turn right, then right again, below the Old Rectory (1744). Walk
down Churchgate, past the parish church of St. Mary's, to the
Market Place (2).

Walk either side of, or through, the covered market. Leave the
Market Place down the narrow, stone paved Bridge Street Brow.
Ahead, Bridge Street leads to the site of the ancient Lancashire
Bridge, now lost as the River Mersey flows under the shopping
precinct and other developments.

Our route lies to the left at the bottom of Bridge Street Brow, along Great Underbank. Until the 19th century, traffic heading south from Manchester would pass this way, having crossed Lancashire Bridge. Tudor Underbank Hall (formerly the town house of the Ardernes of Harden Hall, Bredbury) is to the right.

Continue ahead across the turning circle. The timbered building on the right, now the 3 Shires Wine Bar, may have been part of the town house of the Leghs of Adlington Hall.

Take the walkway on the left which leads straight up across the cliff which forms the valley wall. Air raid shelters were burrowed into the soft sandstone – the entrance to the Air Raid Shelters Museum lies below, on Chestergate. At the top of the walkway, on the left in St Peter's Square, is the statue of Richard Cobden, MP for Stockport 1841-7, and advocate of free trade.

From the top of the walkway, continue ahead to return to the lower level at Mersey Square. The river was covered over here in an "improvement" scheme of the 1930s. Arches carry Wellington Road over the valley and river. Wellington Road, south and north of the river, was built in the mid 1820s as a two mile Stockport by-pass, running then for the most part through fields.

Continue along Chestergate, passing under the first road arch on the left. Beyond, Wellington Road Mill (cotton, 1830) houses the new hatting museum which commemorates an important Stockport industry, with its roots in the 16th century.

Walk on as far as Exchange Street. Here you get a good impression of the length (512m) as well as the height (34m above the river) of the 27 arch railway viaduct (1839-40; widened 1887-9). Turn left into Exchange Street, then climb the stepped path on the right, and turn right at the top, onto Station Road. The Grand Central leisure complex is built on the old railway coal yards site. Walk past the station entrance, then follow the road around to the left.

At the traffic lights, turn right onto Wellington Road South. To the left is Stockport Town Hall (opened 1908); to the right are the former Infirmary (centre portion of facade: 1832) and, across Greek Street, the War Memorial Art Gallery (opened 1925).

Turn left at the top end of the town hall into Edward Street. At traffic lights, Edward Street meets Hillgate, the main route into Stockport from the south before Wellington Road was opened. A diversion of a few hundred yards to the right, along Middle Hillgate, will bring you to the house occupied by cotton manufacturer Samuel Oldknow from 1784 to 1794, before he migrated to Mellor to found an industrial community. In the 19th century the Oldknow house was incorporated into Christie's extensive hatworks.

Return to the junction of Edward Street and Hillgate. Turn right into Waterloo Road, then left (between car parks) into **Hopes Carr (3)**. Walk past the old factory buildings, then turn left into Wellington Street, and right into Lower Hillgate. Robinsons brewery (est. 1854) looms on the right.

At the bottom of Lower Hillgate, bear left into Little Underbank. At the iron span of St. Petersgate Bridge, climb the steps on the

right which lead up to the market place. From here, retrace your steps toward Woodbank Park. Time can be saved by cutting out the Vernon Park stretch: when you reach New Zealand Road, turn right, then left into Turncroft Lane, and enter Woodbank Park at the top of the hill.

1. VERNON PARK

The landowner Lord Vernon offered this site (known as Stringer's Fields) to Stockport Council as a place for public walks and outdoor exercise in 1844, but it was not until 1857 that Stockport's first public park was opened here. Many councillors were not easily persuaded of the need to improve the working class by the provision of wholesome recreational facilities. The council was eventually pushed into action by its own Market Committee, which bought 47,000 trees and shrubs for a bargain price at auction in 1857.

Vernon Park opened on Monday 20 September 1858. An estimated 30,000 people arrived at the park. Two Russian cannon which had been captured in the recent Crimean war fired 21 rounds from the high ground: they were answered by hundreds of cannons around the district. The Choral Society, 400 strong, sang the Hallelujah Chorus. In the evening, bonfires and fireworks could be seen all over the town.

Mill workers subscribed to build fountains. Stockport's two MPs paid for the museum in the park, which opened in 1860. Later additions included a bandstand (1886), a conservatory (1904), and bowling greens (1905, 1908). From 1901, visitors could arrive by electric tram.

At its Edwardian zenith, Vernon Park had up to 60,000 visitors per year. After the Second World War, Vernon Park became depleted, dilapidated and forlorn. Its 100th anniversary was not celebrated at all. In 2000, however, a thorough restoration of the Park was undertaken.

2. MARKET PLACE

The market place, with the parish church at one end and the site of the castle at the other, is likely to have been at the centre of the original Stockport settlement. When that settlement first occurred has been much debated. 19th century antiquarians were convinced that the Romans had a fort here, overlooking the Mersey crossing on which several Roman roads appeared to converge. There is no written record of the castle, or the town, until 1173. The market charter was awarded in 1260. But the very name Stockport, derived from the Old English words for hamlet and market, seems to imply Anglo-Saxon origins.

After 1260, Stockport's market flourished to such an extent that markets as far away as Macclesfield felt threatened. In the early 17th century William Webb wrote that Stockport had "a great market, much frequented by dwellers far remote." In 1795, John Aikin noted that great quantities of corn and oat meal were sold at the weekly market, held on Fridays, which was also "accounted the best market for cheese" in all Cheshire.

Lord Vernon, the lord of the manor, sold his right to regulate the market and collect tolls and rents to Stockport Town Council in 1850. The council built a new classically-fronted market hall (1851), levelled the old castle site which had until recently been occupied by an early cotton mill to form a cattle market (1853), and built the covered market (1860). In 1868, St Petersgate Bridge was built across Little Underbank to provide easier access from the west.

3. HOPES CARR MILLS

Water powered textile mills turned Stockport into an industrial town in the 18th century. Sites were found along the Goyt, Tame and Mersey, and also on smaller streams such as the Tin Brook which flows down the Carrs valley.

Silk throwing was Stockport's first factory industry. The first mill was built by the Mersey upstream from Lancashire Bridge in the 1730s. The second was built in the Carrs in the 1750s. By 1773, according to a parliamentary committee, Stockport had four large silk mills, and other smaller mills, employing around 1,600 hands (more than a third of the population).

In the 1780s the silk mill in the Carrs was converted to cotton spinning, as were other silk mills. New cotton mills were built. John Corry wrote in 1815 that Stockport and vicinity had forty large buildings occupied by cotton spinners. The Middle and Lower Carr Mills on Hopes Carr were built around the late 1820s; they appear to be the oldest surviving cotton mills in Stockport.

Steam had begun to replace water power, factories were growing larger as well as more numerous, and areas such as Hillgate teemed with hastily erected cottages and tenements. By 1844, Frederick Engels could write that "Stockport presents a truly revolting picture... notoriously one of the darkest and smokiest holes in the whole industrial area." **LE**

Swettenham

A535 from Chelford (& Macclesfield and Wilmslow)

Cranage the Hermitage

River Dane

A54 from Congleton

Holmes Chapel Station

① The Ironmaster's Bridge
② Saltersford
③ Swettenham

N

LENGTH OF WALK: Approximately seven miles.

DEGREE OF DIFFICULTY: Low.

PUBLIC TRANSPORT: Holmes Chapel Station is on the railway line from Manchester, Stockport and Wilmslow to Sandbach and Crewe. A bus service from Sandbach runs through Holmes Chapel.

ORDNANCE SURVEY MAP: At 1:25,000, this walk can be found on Pathfinder map 775 (Winsford and Sandbach), but the western extremity of the walk, through Swettenham village, is on Pathfinder map 776 (Congleton).

We begin this walk in Holmes Chapel, once a coaching halt on the great road from London to Carlisle (and known then as Church Hulme). We follow a side road down to the River Dane, which we cross on the picturesque Hermitage Bridge, built in the early 18th century by the master of Cranage ironworks, situated downstream. The waymarks of the Dane Valley Way guide us along the northern banks of the Dane. Beyond the mighty red brick railway viaduct which spans the valley close to the spot where medieval salters forded the Dane with their packhorse trains, a rather difficult crossing of a main road with fast moving traffic has to be made, but thereafter we walk in deep rural isolation, climbing high above the Dane and its tributary, the Swettenham Brook. We descend through the Swettenham Meadows Nature Reserve, cross the brook, and enter the quiet cul-de-sac village of Swettenham, perhaps calling at the Swettenham Arms, tucked away behind the church of St. Peter. The road ends at the Dragon's Cave, an estate gatehouse. A bridle track takes us to an iron bridge over the Dane, and we return towards Holmes Chapel through woods and fields on the southern side of the river.

This walk begins in Holmes Chapel, once a coaching halt on the great road from London to Carlisle (and known then as Church Hulme). Beyond the Red Lion and St. Luke's Church, turn right into Macclesfield Road (the A 535). After about a quarter of a mile, turn left into Hermitage Drive, and continue along the track at the bottom down to the River Dane and Hermitage Bridge, the **Ironmaster's Bridge (1)**.

Cross the bridge and turn right into the riverside fields. The path follows the riverbank for a while, before cutting across the field toward the left end of a row of trees, following the river loop around to the right, and passing under the railway viaduct. The path climbs an embankment to the A 535, close to the bridge over the Dane which probably marks the site of the ancient **Saltersford (2)**.

Turn left. There is no alternative to walking alongside the main road for about a quarter of a mile. For about two hundred yards there is a narrow footpath. After that, walk on the grass verge until it disappears, then cross to the lay-by and verge on the other side. Traffic moves fast here, so be very careful, especially when crossing back over to the waymarked field path which starts at a hedge stile on the right hand side of the road, a few yards further on. This crossing is just in front of a blind bend around which traffic travels too fast. It is a shame that the Dane Valley Way has to include this danger spot: perhaps one day the roadside footpath will be extended this far.

Once in the field, walk directly ahead, keeping the hedge to your left. Beyond a stile high above a bend in the river the path follows the line of the river for a few feet before crossing a field, then descending to cross a stream in a narrow strip of woodland. Climb out of the wood, and walk ahead between cultivated fields. The path is overgrown, but it should be discernible.

In front of a wood on the other side, turn left and walk up an earth track. Around the corner at the top, take the signed path on the right, keeping the woods to your right for a hundred yards or so, then cross the stile and walk down through the woods to cross a stream by a plank bridge. Signs and stiles show the way up the bank and through the fields beyond.

After passing a small pool on the left, turn left, walk up the rise, and cross a stile. The path swings to the right and runs along the top edge of Greenhey Wood, and then (over another stile) continues ahead along the top of a steep bank above the Swettenham Brook.

Continue straight ahead past farm out-buildings and along a tarred farm road to Brook Farm, and on along a grassed track to Ashtree Farm. Continue ahead on what is now a surfaced track. After about a quarter of a mile, take the signed path on the right down through the Swettenham Meadows Nature Reserve. Cross the brook on a wooden bridge, and climb the bank, bearing right, to join a quiet lane. Turn right, and walk along the lane into **Swettenham (3)**. Follow the road round to the left in front of the telephone box/bus stop. Behind St. Peter's Church can be seen the Swettenham Arms – known to some as the Swetty Arms.

Walk on to the end of the lane. Go through the gate next to the 'Dragon's Cave' into the Davenport Hall estate. Follow the bridleway, which crosses the Dane on a modern iron bridge. After a straight stretch of track across the river meadows, go through the wooden gate on the right, and follow the path which climbs through woodland to the top of a high bank above the river. There are some precipitous dips and muddy patches here. The path follows the edge of the woods for a while, then descends through woods to river level. Bear left, and walk through a field to a loop in the river. There is a muddy patch here – you may find it easiest to pass at the very edge of the river.

Walk across the field beyond to a gate by a stream. A permissive path for anglers follows the meanders of the river, but the right of way crosses the stream, climbs the bank to a stile, then bears right around the hillside before continuing straight ahead, with a fence to the right. Continue straight on through a gate, across the bottom of a concrete track, and through another gate. Walk on, with the fence and woods to your left, then bear right across the field to a white footpath sign on the margin of a belt of trees ahead.

The path leads down through trees, crosses a stream by a plank, and climbs out of the trees to a stile. Over the stile, turn sharp left to join a track which climbs up out of the valley. The route can now be described very simply: we merely follow this track for about a mile, to emerge at Saltersford Corner on the A535. Turn left here, and carry straight on if you wish to return to the centre of Holmes Chapel. To return more directly to the railway station, make another turn left into Manor Lane, at the bottom of which, turn right.

1. THE IRONMASTER'S BRIDGE

A weathered inscription on Hermitage Bridge shows that it was built in 1707 by Thomas Hall, ironmaster, and rebuilt (perhaps after flood damage?) by Edward Hall. Thomas Hall (1657-1715) lived in the Hermitage, a large and ancient mansion above the north bank of the Dane, which he rebuilt and extended in or around 1707. He was a member of various partnerships which controlled the Cheshire iron industry, which had grown rapidly since the middle of the 17th century.

Half a mile downstream, below Cranage bridge which carried the great road from London to Carlisle over the Dane, lay the Cranage Forge and Slitting Mill, which had been taken over by Thomas Hall and William Cotton in 1696. To Cranage came pig iron which had been smelted (using Staffordshire and Cumbrian ores) in furnaces at Vale Royal, Church Lawton, and in North Staffordshire. In the Cranage Forge finery and chafery the pig was converted into workable bar iron, and in the slitting mill some of it was slit into rods for the use of nailmakers. Sales

the river Dane from the Hermitage Bridge

books for the period 1696 to 1710 show that Cranage bar iron and rods were sold over a wide area, bounded by Newcastle Under Lyme, Wrexham, Liverpool, Warrington, Macclesfield and Congleton.

A recently published history of this area comments that the existence deep in rural Cheshire of an iron industry which was of national significance for around a hundred years "is perhaps a surprising fact" (*A Journey Through Time – Holmes Chapel, Cotton and Cranage.* 1996). The iron industry was widely dispersed in disintegrated rural units because of its voracious appetite for timber, which was used to make charcoal fuel for the furnaces and for some forge processes. Cranage was an excellent centre for the distribution of iron to the scattered manufacturers of iron wares because it was connected to Newcastle and Warrington by the great north road, and was close to branch roads (at Holmes Chapel) to Middlewich and Chester, and to Macclesfield and Congleton, and (a little further north) to Manchester.

2. SALTERSFORD

The salters who forded the Dane near Holmes Chapel were carrying salt by pack horse trains from the salt works at Middlewich into east Cheshire, and across the Peak into Yorkshire. The trade in salt, which was used in food preservation and in tanning, was well developed in Anglo-Saxon times, and the routes taken by the salters probably became established then, if not earlier.

W. B. Crump showed how place names allow us to reconstruct the various Saltways from the Cheshire Wiches (*Transactions of the Lancashire and Cheshire Antiquarian Society*, 1939). The route of the carriers of salt from Middlewich (joined no doubt by carriers from Northwich) can be picked up at Saltersford in the hills near Rainow, above Macclesfield, and followed through another Saltersford near Tideswell, and another at Owler Bar above Sheffield. An alternative route lay further north in the Hope Valley, where we find Salto Lane and Salter Barn near Castleton, and Saltergate Lane near Bamford.

The name of the Saltersford near Holmes Chapel seems to have been first recorded in 1331 when Edward III granted "pontage for five years on wares passing over the River Davena [Dane] between Macclesfield and Middlewich to build a stone bridge at Salteresford." The bridge became the responsibility of the county, and was rebuilt around 1719, and again later. The significance of the bridge is somewhat obscured by the causeway on either side, and it is now overshadowed by the great viaduct of the Manchester and Birmingham Railway's line between Manchester and Crewe, which was opened in 1842. With 23 arches this was the longest viaduct on the line, though that at Stockport is slightly higher.

The population of Holmes Chapel doubled while the viaduct was being constructed. A navvy encampment occupied the valley. The culture shock must have been terrific, but unfortunately no colourful tales of camp life seem to have been recorded.

3. SWETTENHAM

When Cliff Rathbone, "Stroller" of the *Macclesfield Times and Courier*, visited the Swettenham Arms in 1953, the pub stood "in a farmyard with hens and ducks feeding almost up to the front door." Mrs Hankey, the landlady, dispensed both beer and village lore: the inn was in medieval times a nunnery, connected to the church by a secret underground passage. The village, said Mrs Hankey, was formerly haunted by the ghost of a nun, murdered for breaking her vow of chastity. The haunting had ceased after absolution was recited each night over a period of two weeks.

Hair-raising though the ghostly nun may have been, the villagers of Swettenham in days gone by had many more tangible problems. Rabies appears to have been one of these: the churchwardens recorded in their accounts for 1745 receipts for two methods of curing "the bite of A mad Dogg or Catt."

The first involved doses of cinnibar and "best Musk", taken frequently in "a tea cup full of Arrak or, if not to be had, in the same quantity of French brandy." This was described as "never failing". Nonetheless, an alternative was given shortly afterwards, made with rue, garlic, and "mothridato, or Venice treacle", boiled in old ale, to which "adde a handfull of Asli coloured liverwort" and give warm "to a man that is bit" but cold to beasts. **LE**

St Peter's Church, Swettenham

Three Shire Heads:
The Upper Goyt Valley

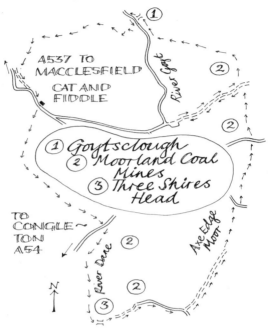

Length of Walk: Approximately 10 miles.

Public Transport: The Cat and Fiddle Inn on this walk can be reached by bus from Macclesfield and Buxton. You can also walk from Buxton and join the route at Burbage, and taking the old road to Macclesfield – a distance of about two miles from Buxton Railway Station.

Ordnance Survey Map: At 1:25,000, this walk can be found on Outdoor Leisure map no. 24: The Peak District, White Peak Area.

This walk takes you into three counties: Cheshire, Derbyshire and Staffordshire. The full walk is a circuit of the highest moorlands of the western Peak. On a fine day, panoramic views in different directions include the gritstone plateau of Kinder Scout, the Cheshire plain and the Welsh mountains, Shutlingslow, Bosley Cloud, the Roaches, Ramshaw Rocks, and the limestone plateau of the central Peak. Much of the walk is at 500 metres or thereabouts, but we follow packhorse trails down to packhorse bridges across the infant rivers Goyt and Dane. Traces of a surprising amount of past economic activity can be seen.

Coal mining took place on the most isolated moorland: keep clear
of the depressions which may indicate former mineshafts. Most of
the paths used are fairly clear, but it would be unwise to attempt
this walk in misty weather.

This walk starts at the car park and information centre near
Derbyshire Bridge at the head of the Goyt Valley. Access is from
the A 537 Macclesfield-Buxton road, signed Derbyshire Bridge.
The car park near Derbyshire Bridge is on the site of Goyt's
Moss Farm, one of four small farms in the immediate vicinity.
All were demolished in the 1930s when Fernilee Reservoir was
built downstream.

From the car park, walk up the stone track, which was the
first turnpike road between Macclesfield and Buxton, authorised
by Act of Parliament in 1758. After about three-quarters of a
mile, at the top of the hill, Buxton can be seen below. This point
is on the watershed of England: while the Goyt flows into the
Mersey and the Irish Sea, the streams which run down to
Buxton become the Wye, and eventually reach the North Sea.

Take the waymarked path on the left, which follows the
moorland ridge for about five hundred metres, then swings left
to follow Berry Clough down into the Goyt Valley. Just before
the wooden bridge cross the Goyt, turn right and follow the path
along the right hand bank, through the bracken. The path
passes above the stone packhorse bridge at **Goytsclough (1)**,
then twists back down to it.

Cross the bridge and climb up to the road. Take the track
immediately opposite, which turns to the left in front of the site
of Goytsclough Mill, then turns right as it climbs toward a
plantation of pines, crossing the overgrown mill leat on the way.
Walk for a few yards with the trees on your right, and then take
the path to the right which leads through and along the top edge
of the plantation for about three quarters of a mile. Where a
track comes up out of the trees, cross straight over it and follow
the path, which climbs the ridge ahead quite steeply.

At the top take the path to the left, which joins a track which
is the line of the 1758 turnpike (bear left). The old road joins the
new Macclesfield-Buxton turnpike line authorised by Act in
1821, now the A537. Walk carefully alongside the main road for
a few yards up to the Cat and Fiddle.

Take the well-marked pathway which begins directly opposite
the pub, and crosses the moors for a mile and a half, leading to
the A54 Congleton-Buxton road (formerly a turnpike, authorised
by Act of 1789). Cross straight over the road, watching out
especially for traffic from the right. Step over the low crash
barrier, and follow the rough path which drops steeply down to
the infant River Dane. The stone chimney on the hillside was
connected by a flue to a steam engine, which may have been
used to drive an endless rope haulage system in the Dane Bower
Colliery – **Moorland Coal Mines (2)**. Follow the grassy track
downstream. Overgrown spoil heaps can be seen on the right.

Further on, the path passes close by the stonework of an adit (horizontal) entrance to the colliery, next to the stream.

Continue to walk downstream as far as the packhorse bridge at **Three Shire Heads (3)**. Cross the bridge and take the path which lies straight ahead, through an iron gate. After a few hundred yards the track splits: keep to the left, following the stream towards Blackclough. The tiny homesteads of former moorland farmers, miners and button makers dot the hillsides. Where the track becomes a narrow tarred road continue ahead, ignoring farm tracks to the right and left.

Near the top of the valley the road twists sharply to the right. At this point carry straight on along a stone track, until it turns to the left towards Orchard Farm. Continue ahead on the more grassy track. After about half a mile, past overgrown quarry workings on the left, look out for a small concrete obelisk (which perhaps marks a capped mineshaft) on the right. Nearby, but on the left of the track, is a faintly visible field path. Follow this up to the convergence of stone walls from the right and from the left. This is the most northerly point of Staffordshire.

Follow the path ahead across the Derbyshire moorland to a minor road. Turn right onto the road, then almost immediately left onto a waymarked path and continue across the moors, past spoil heaps and shafts connected to the Thatch Marsh colliery. Walk down to the main road, cross straight over, and continue ahead to the stone trackway of the 1758 turnpike. Turn left and return to the starting point.

1. GOYTSCLOUGH

Where the deep Clough stream meets the Goyt, Goytsclough has an interestingly dishevelled look, with tumbled stones, oddly shaped grassy mounds, mysterious trackways and water channels, and faint traces of ruined buildings, which indicate long vanished industrial activity.

An east-west packhorse trail crossed the Goyt here, though the present packhorse bridge was moved up the valley from Goytsbridge when the Errwood Reservoir was constructed in the 1960s. The quarries to the west of the road at Goytsclough were worked in the 17th century by Thomas Pickford, reputed to be a founder of Pickfords the carriers. Stone was carried out by packhorse; general carrying developed, it is said, to fill the empty panniers on the return journey.

By the early 19th century, water from the Goyt and from Deep Clough was used to power a stone saw mill which stood beside the Deep Clough stream, near to the road. By the late 19th century the mill was being used for crushing barytes for use in paint. Leats along the hillsides fed a pool above the mill – a waterfall indicates the site, which is today occupied by a covered reservoir built in the 1930s to supply water to the high districts around Disley. At this time, Stockport Corporation demolished the remains of the mill, the row of cottages which stood opposite and nearby Goytsclough Farm.

2. MOORLAND COAL MINES

Thin coal seams lie between sandstones and shales under these moors. The coal was used for domestic fires and by the Peak limeburners until railways brought better coal into the district cheaply. Physical evidence of the mines is easy to find on close inspection. Small depressions, some filled with water, mark the site of bell pits or shafts. Nearby spoil mounds and horse gin circles may be seen. Overgrown trackways lead to packhorse trails and the turnpike roads. In the valleys drainage sloughs and adit entrances lead back into deeper mines.

evidence of Moorland coal mines

Their working lives must have been hard, but miners may have been a philosophical breed. In the 1860s William Beresford reported that the colliers of the Dane and Blackclough mines, which were connected, "used sometimes to meet underground and smoke their pipes together." The colliers' cottages on the dreary moors, he wrote, "are generally as ugly and low as possible, and seem to be hugging the ground to avoid the winds ... still, you will generally find a white apron and a clean floor, and smiling faces."

3. THREE SHIRE HEADS

Cheshire, Derbyshire and Staffordshire meet at the point where the tributary stream from Blackclough enters the Dane. Packhorse trails from the three counties converged here. Three Shires Bridge was originally a narrow packhorse bridge, as a glance at the underside of the arch will show. Below the bridge is Panniers Pool, where the packhorses would be watered, and perhaps relieved of their panniers while resting.

The moorlands on the Staffordshire side, and around the village of Flash, were home to many a well-travelled pedlar and hawker, trading in locally produced buttons, silk ribbons from Leek, and Manchester smallwares. William Beresford wrote in the 1860s that "a grey haired few of them still linger on, still smoke their pipes in chimney corners, and now and then tell tales of their adventures ... No one should, therefore, be surprised if he heard an old Moorlander comparing the various merits of Berwick or Brighton, or telling of some similar adventures which he met with on the mountains of Merioneth, or the fens of Lincoln." LE

Three Shire Heads Bridge

Tideswell to Cressbrook Dale

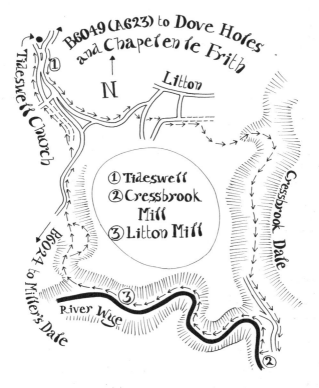

B6049 (A623) to Dove Holes and Chapel en le Frith

N

Litton

Tideswell Church

B6024 to Miller's Dale

River Wye

Cressbrook Dale

① Tideswell
② Cressbrook Mill
③ Litton Mill

LENGTH OF WALK: Approximately 7 miles.
DIFFICULTY RATING: Low
ORDNANCE SURVEY MAP: At 1:25,000, this walk can be found on the Outdoor Leisure Map No. 24, The Peak District, White Peak Area.
PUBLIC TRANSPORT: Bus services are available to Tideswell from Buxton.

This walk begins in Tideswell, a textile and market town which was once prosperous, but which the Industrial Revolution passed by. We descend past old lead mine workings into Cressbrook Dale, which in turn gives access to the Wye Valley. Here are two water-powered cotton mill sites, separated by a dramatic limestone gorge. Both of these remote mills used, and probably abused, pauper apprentices who were sometimes hundreds of miles from their homes. The return to Tideswell is made past the basalt quarry in Tideswell Dale, where a volcano spewed lava into the shallow tropical sea in which the limestone was laid down some three hundred million years ago.

This walk begins at the parish church of **Tideswell (1)**, on Commercial Road. From the church, walk through the centre of the town by Church Street or Queen Street. The road widens out at Fountain Square: continue along the left hand side for about a quarter of a mile.

Just after the roadside footpath ends, turn left onto the narrow road which rises above and follows the main road down the dale, then swings left toward Litton village, and joins a more important branch from the main road. Turn left here and walk toward Litton for a quarter of a mile or so (there is a footpath). Before the first house on the right, take the (signed) footpath which leads up a grassy hillside. Cross straight over the minor road at the top. The path crosses a small field, then swings left to cross a second field diagonally, then right to follow a wall, passing through a series of stiles in intersecting walls. Between the path and the village of Litton to the left are Townside Closes – long narrow fields of old enclosure, connected to the farms which lined the Litton village street. The open fields, which were enclosed in the 1760s, lay to the right.

Continue ahead when the path joins a tarred road, but when the road swings left toward Litton carry straight on along a stony walled track. After about 250 yards climb the steps in the wall on the right and pass down a narrow field. Bear left where the field widens and walk down into Tansley Dale. Disturbed ground and spoil heaps indicate the former workings of Harbourseats lead mine.

Tansley Dale opens into Cressbrook Dale. Turn right and walk down into the valley. The right of way lies along the path which climbs up the hillside, and returns to the valley bottom a little further on. However, there is a well-worn path leading directly down the valley. Mounds and stonework mark the sites of lead mine soughs (or drainage tunnels).

Walk on through trees and bushes for half a mile or so, cross the footbridge, and follow the streamside path for another quarter of a mile to Ravensdale Cottages, which were built in 1823 for workers at **Cressbrook Mill (2)**. From the cottages, a tarred track climbs to a minor road. Cressbrook Mill is at the bottom of the hill, on the right. Turn right in front of the first mill building.

Walk between the mill and a former apprentice house, which is above the bank on the right. The path swings to the right, crosses the mill leat, and passes beneath the limestone cliff of Water-cum-Jolly Dale. Reeds and water fowl have colonised the river which here forms a mill pool. The path to **Litton Mill (3)** is concessionary, though it forms part of the Monsal Trail. Half a mile on, a small water wheel once pumped water to the settlement of Cressbrookdale, high above. An iron sheeting bridge crosses the tail race from Litton Mill. The path passes between the disused mill buildings.

Walk between the mill buildings and then follow the road between the cottages on the right and the mill pool on the left. Two hundred yards or so beyond the cottages take the path on the right through the trees, which leads up through Tideswell Dale. Where the path divides, take the right hand branch which crosses the stream.

If you wish to see the site of the basalt quarry, you can make a detour on a path on the right, which leads by steps to the top of grassed over spoil heaps, passes the quarry face, and returns into Tideswell Dale. Continue up the valley. Beyond the information centre and car park, follow the path under a row of beech trees to the road. Cross over, and walk along the roadside path to the far end of the (delightfully situated) sewage works. The roadside path leads back to Tideswell, but to avoid the road, you can take the field path on the left which climbs the valley side, joining a track which also leads back to Tideswell.

1. TIDESWELL

Tideswell's impressive 14th century parish church, the 'Cathedral of the Peak', is an indication of the past importance of the town. It is likely that local sheep farming and the woollen trades, together with lead mining, were responsible for Tideswell's medieval prosperity. The ancient feast of 'Bishop Blaze', who was torn to death with iron combs in AD316 and became the patron saint of wool-combers, was still celebrated here in the 19th century.

The town's textile trades by now included wool and silk weaving, fustian cutting and flax dressing, but enterprises were mostly small scale, much production was domestic, and wages were low. Tideswell, high on the limestone uplands, lacked the streams necessary for the water powered factories of the early Industrial Revolution.

The contrast between Tideswell's late 19th century poverty and its former prosperity is perhaps what led topographical writers such as James Croston (*On Foot Through the Peak* 1862) to emphasise the "poor and mean looking dwellings" and the alleged idiocy of the 'Tidser' folk, who were said to put wire netting around their gardens to keep out the smallpox, to put tallow candles in the oven to dry, and so on.

2. CRESSBROOK MILL

The first cotton spinning mill on this site was built for Richard Arkwright in 1783. The elegant 'Big Mill' on the left of the path was put up in 1814-15. Further buildings followed, including weaving sheds on the south side of the complex in the 1880s. Water for the wheels came from the Wye itself which was dammed, and from pools on the Cress Brook. Cotton production continued here until 1965.

In the early years of Cressbrook Mill, it was found necessary to employ several hundred pauper apprentices at any one time. Their treatment under William Newton, mill manager and poet, has traditionally been described as exemplary. Visiting JPs do seem to have considered the housing, clothing, feeding and education of the apprentices more than adequate. But the justices did not concern themselves with discipline. Appalling floggings administered by the mill overseers and by Newton were described by two apprentices, a boy from a London workhouse and a girl from Bristol workhouse. Mr Newton had beaten two apprentices so severely about their heads, wrote the Bristol girl, that they died. She herself was so "feared and dateless" from the punishment she had received that for a long time after her release she was "like a person with no wits".

These accounts were published twenty to thirty years after the events, in a radical newspaper which was campaigning for factory reform. There appears to be no supporting evidence. But we should at least be wary of claims that Newton showed at Cressbrook Mill that the pauper apprentice system could operate humanely.

3. LITTON MILL

A cotton spinning mill was built here, on the site of an old corn mill, in 1782. Ellis Needham ran the mill with various partners until his bankruptcy in 1815. Before he died fifteen years later Needham had become notorious for his alleged ill treatment of the many pauper apprentices employed here. One of them, Robert Blincoe, told his story to a journalist, and the resulting 'Memoir of Robert Blincoe'

Cressbrook Mill

was published in a radical journal and as a pamphlet during the factory reform agitation of the 1820s and 1830s.

Blincoe told of excessive hours of work, overcrowded and unhealthy lodgings and inadequate food. Magistrates' reports provide some support for Blincoe on these points. But the best known passages in the memoir describe physical atrocities. Blincoe claimed that the overseers and other adult workers continually and viciously beat the apprentices, forced them to eat dirty pieces of candle and lick up tobacco spittle, and filed their teeth. Blincoe had been suspended in agony over moving machinery. Needham, far from restraining his overseers, "used to animate them by his own example to inflict punishment in any and every way they pleased. Mr Needham stands accused of having been in the habit of knocking down the apprentices with his clenched fists, kicking them about when down, beating them to excess with sticks, or flogging them with horse whips; of seizing them by the ears, lifting them from the ground and forcibly dashing them down on the floor, and pinching them until his nails met." The surviving mill buildings mostly belong to later periods – the mill was rebuilt after a fire in 1874. Textile production continued here until 1974. LE

Warrington
and Stockton Heath

LENGTH OF WALK: Approximately 7 miles.
DEGREE OF DIFFICULTY: Easy.
ORDNANCE SURVEY MAPS: At 1:25000, this walk can be found on Pathfinder maps 740 (Warrington) and 739 (Widnes).

This walk is a circuit of some of Warrington's once busy, now much altered, waterways. We start near the point where the mighty Manchester Ship Canal cut across the older Runcorn and Latchford Canal. The filled-in course of the latter, now the Black Bear Linear Park, is followed to the remains of the lock at which the canal joined the Mersey. We walk along the Mersey bank, cross the river on a lively suspension footbridge, and pass by former quays and an abandoned lock. From Warrington Bridge we cut through the town centre and then walk past railway marshalling yards to rejoin the Mersey near Bank Quay. We now begin our return journey, walking at the river's edge before crossing on a footbridge attached to a railway bridge, inches away from the tracks. We return to the Ship Canal alongside a defunct canal, and past overgrown and abandoned river channels.

A suitable starting place for this walk is Stockton Heath, a suburb about a mile and a quarter to the south of Warrington town centre, on the A49, known here as London Road. It should not be difficult to find a parking place close to the crossroads at the centre of this urban village.

Walk down London Road toward Warrington, and cross the swing bridge over the **Manchester Ship Canal (1)**. Take the path on the right immediately beyond the bridge, and enter the **Black Bear Linear Park (2)**. The Trans-Pennine Trail bears off to the right, following the Ship Canal; we carry on ahead along the route of the former Runcorn and Latchford Canal, following the signs for Kingsway Bridge.

The track passes under Loushers Lane, then under the high iron bridge of the former Warrington and Altrincham Junction Railway (opened 1854). Further on, Black Bear Bridge (rebuilt 1926) carries Knutsford Road over the former canal. Beyond, Victoria Park (opened 1897) can be seen on the left.

At the point where the canal joined the River Mersey, are the remains of Manor Lock. Kingsway Bridge (opened 1935) is to the right.

We turn left at Manor Lock, and follow the path along the bank of the Mersey. On the opposite bank were sited some of the tanneries for which Warrington was renowned in the early 20th century. Further on, the Old Quay Inn marks the site of the once-busy Howley Quay.

Cross the river on the Howley Suspension Footbridge. "Swinging or jumping on this bridge strictly forbidden" a notice tells us, and with good reason. This bridge can rival London's Millennium Bridge as a mover and shaker.

Go down the steps on the right, then follow the riverside path round under the foot bridge. After a few hundred yards the river sweeps around a horse shoe bend, the site of an ancient ford. Howley Lock, which forms a cut-off, was the first lock on the Mersey and Irwell Navigation (see 2). Below the weir the river is tidal.

Continue along the riverside path. Below the lock stood the Mersey Corn Mill, with a water wheel fed by a leat from the river above the lock. Further on was the Warrington Corporation Electricity Station (opened 1900, demolished 1983). A 'convey' brought coal from railway sidings, passing under Knutsford Road and across the river to the plant.

The riverside path joins a riverside road, Wharf Street. Ahead lies the new Warrington Bridge (opened 1987), on the site of Bishop's Wharf. Beyond, on the site occupied by bridges since the middle ages, and for most of that time the lowest bridging point on the Mersey, is the 'New Bridge' built 1913-15.

We must aim for the brick buildings of the former Warrington Academy (1757-1786; a non-conformist university in all but name), which can be seen across the immense traffic roundabout of which the two bridges now form a part. A system of pelican crossings gives some protection.

In front of the Academy buildings turn right into Bridge Street, then second left into Rylands Street. Our route lies straight ahead, but to the right, along Cairo Street, can be seen the 18th century

Warrington Town Hall

Unitarian chapel attended by students and tutors of the Academy; on the left, down Bold Street, is the municipal museum (founded 1848; present Museum and Art gallery building erected 1857).

Continue ahead along Palmyra Square. Queen's Gardens (1897) and the Boer War Memorial are to the right; Parr Hall (1895) and the Technical School (1902) are on the left. At the end of the gardens, turn right into Springfield Street. At the top turn left into Sankey Street.

On the right, behind the recently restored "golden gates" is Bank Hall, built in 1750 by industrialist Thomas Patten and used as Warrington Town Hall since 1872.

Walk along Sankey Street to the traffic lights and turn left into Parker Street. On the right is Bank Quay Station. **Bank Quay (3)**, on the Mersey, lay behind the soapworks (formerly Crossfield's) which looms over the station.

Beyond the station, follow the road round to the left, then turn right into Slutchers Lane. A bridge crosses railway lines. To the left, a short way down the line to Altrincham and Stockport, lay Arpley Station; to the right was Bank Quay Low Level Station. Both have now disappeared.

Turn right on the top of the bridge over the rail lines. Follow the road past Arpley Marshalling Yards (opened 1900), round to the left, then right under the 'West Coast' main railway line. On the other side, follow the tarmac surfaced track to the left. At the top of the rise opposite the dog and cat sanctuary, take the path on the left which follows a fence across flat open land to the river. Note over to the right the framework of a transporter bridge built in 1916 to connect parts of Crossfields works which lay on opposite sides of the river. Uniquely, this transporter bridge was built to carry rail vehicles.

The path drops down to the Mersey. Take the waymarked path to the left, along the river edge. This path is presently rather neglected and overgrown. Persist, and after half a mile or so, having passed under the railway, you will be rewarded by a rather exciting river crossing made on a footbridge attached to the second railway bridge, at the level of the rails.

Having crossed the river, turn left, following the Trans-Pennine Trail along the riverside. The main river swings away, occupying a cut made in the late 19th century across Arpley Meadows. To the left now is the muddy overgrown original channel. On the right is a surviving stretch of the Runcorn and Latchford Canal.

The path emerges onto Chester Road. Turn left and cross the bridge over the river channel, then take the path on the right, following the Trans-Pennine waymarkers. Walton Lock, a little way further on, was built to give Ship Canal traffic access to Bank Quay and other Warrington quays on the Mersey. From this point, the old river course which ran parallel to Wilderspool Causeway was blocked off. Follow the trail around to the right, pass in front of a row of brick cottages, then turn left to follow the trail alongside the Ship Canal back to the London Road swingbridge, and return from there to Stockton Heath.

1. MANCHESTER SHIP CANAL

Manchester businessmen, exasperated by high Liverpool dock dues and heavy railway charges, were the driving force behind the Ship Canal. The original plan was to start the canal at Warrington, while dredging a channel deep enough for ocean going ships from there to the Mersey estuary. In the event the canal, 26 feet deep and 120 feet wide, was begun in the estuary at Eastham. It runs along the Cheshire side of the valley to a point above Warrington, before following the former course of the Mersey and then the Irwell to Manchester.

Construction began in 1889; the builders were plagued by floods and accidents. An official of the navvies' union claimed that more than 1,000 men were killed. A representative of the Master Builders Association admitted to 130 killed, 165 'permanently injured' and 997 'slightly injured'.

Our walk crosses part of section 5, Norton to Latchford, for which the contractor was John Jackson. This was described as the worst piece of the canal to deal with, containing as it did the locks and sluices at Latchford, two railway bridges, and five swing bridges.

Attitudes to the canal in Warrington were divided. The transport benefits were not great. The swing bridges held up the traffic. The flow of the Mersey was impeded. It was claimed that the river had become "nothing less than an open sewer, and that people could scarcely live in their houses" (quoted in Bosdin Leech: History of the Manchester Ship Canal, 1907).

Insult was added to injury: Queen Victoria, who opened the Ship Canal in 1894, refused to visit Warrington, and the Warrington authorities were not invited to the Manchester celebration.

2. BLACK BEAR LINEAR PARK

Black Bear Linear Park occupies a filled-in section of the Runcorn and Latchford Canal, which was popularly known as the Black Bear Canal after a pub in Latchford.

The Runcorn and Latchford Canal was a refinement of the Mersey and Irwell Navigation, whose undertakers had first improved these rivers in the 1730s, with locks and short cuts, allowing barges to reach Manchester. Below Howley Lock in Warrington, the river was tidal and naturally navigable - but shallows often delayed the traffic.

When the Bridgewater Canal between Manchester and Runcorn (opened 1776) began to provide competition, the Mersey and Irwell company built the Runcorn and Latchford Canal to by-pass the shallows and shorten the route to Manchester. It was opened in 1804.

The construction of the Ship Canal made the western section of the Runcorn and Latchford Canal redundant, and, at the site of the London Road swing bridge, obliterated it altogether. Immediately to the east of the swing bridge, a lock was built to admit barges from the Ship Canal into the surviving section (which is now the park) allowing them to reach the Mersey at Latchford. By the 1960s the canal was disused, and a death-trap; in the 1970s it was filled in.

3. BANK QUAY

Bank Quay became the commercial and industrial centre of Warrington, once Thomas Patten had the fish weirs of the lower Mersey cleared away in the late 17th century. A century later, John Aiken wrote that "Warrington may be considered a port town, the Mersey admitting, by the help of the tide, vessels of 70 or 80 tons burthen, to Bank-quay, a little below the town, where warehouses, cranes, and other conveniences for landing goods, are erected." (*Description of the Country 30-40 Miles around Manchester*, 1795)

Thomas Patten began copper smelting at Bank Quay around 1717. The roll call of Bank Quay's industries since then indicates the diversity of Warrington's enterprises: it includes wire making, iron works, engineering, including ship building, cotton manufacture, flour milling, glass, chemicals and soap.

Bank Quay is the site of Warrington's principal station. The pioneering Liverpool to Manchester railway (opened 1830) passed to the north of the town, but in 1831 a short connecting line was built from Bank Quay to Newton.

In 1837, the Grand Junction Railway from Birmingham came across the Mersey to connect with the Warrington and Newton line at Bank Quay, for access to Liverpool and to Manchester. More direct lines were soon built, but the railway was continued north from Bank Quay, and Bank Quay Station (on its present site since 1868) now serves the West Coast main line from London to Glasgow.

Stockton Heath

LivingEDGE Book of Walks

Index

CASE BOUND LIMITED EDITIONS

A Sketch of the Parish of Prestbury

by George Yamold Osborne.

Originally published in 1840, Osbourne's book ranges through the 32 townships which originally comprised the far-flung Parish of Prestbury, including:

Adlington, Birtles, Butley, Bollington, Bosley, Capesthorne, Chelford, Falleybroome, Henbury-Cum-Pexhall, Lyme Handley, Marton, Mottram Andrew, Newton, Poynton, North Rode, Siddington, Tytherington, Upton, Old Withington, Lower Withington, Woodford, Worth, Macclesfield, Hurdsfield, Kettleshulme, Wildboarclough, Wincle, Rainow and Pott Shrigley.

Hard cover, with new illustrations.
750 numbered copies
£23 (Presentation edition in slip case £28.50)

Swythamley and its Neighbourhood

by Sir Philip Brocklehurst

FEW ONLY REMAINING

Hard cover, original illustrations.
500 numbered copies £18.95

Scientific Rambles Round Macclesfield

by J D Sainter
with an introduction by Alan Garner

A companion for walkers and country lovers, or anyone with an interest in the flora, fauna, bird life and geology of the land of the Three Shires. Hard cover, newly illustrated.
750 numbered copies £18.95

QUALITY SOFT COVER EDITIONS

The Villas of Alderley Edge
by Matthew Hyde
Recording the expansion of a small Cheshire
village as the 'Cottentots' move in.
Many illustrations. £12.95

A Window on Knutsford
Essays on the Architecture and History of
Knutsfor by Matthew Hyde
A companion volume to *The Villas of Alderley
Edge*, lavishly illustrated and including
previously unpublished extracts from the
sketchbooks of Knutsford architect Richard
Harding Watt. £12.95.

Goostrey Remembered
by Jean Smallwood.
A new book on the village of Goostrey. £9.95.

In Preparation:

A new illustrated edition of
Katherine Chorley's
Manchester Made Them
Due for publication Autumn 2001

TO OBTAIN YOUR COPIES CONTACT SILK PRESS BOOKS ON
0161 928 0333 /0161 929 4884

Or return the order form below to:
Silk Press Books
14a Bath Street, Hale, Cheshire WA14 2EJ

Postage £1.50 each, **5 books or more postage free.**
(UK and EU postal area only)

Name..

Address ....

....

....

Postcode ....

A Sketch of the Parish of Prestbury
£23/£28.50 each Qty ....Total..............................

Swythamley and its Neighbourhood
£18.95 each   Qty ....Total..............................

Scientific Rambles Round Macclesfield
£18.95 each   Qty ....Total..............................

The Villas of Alderley Edge
£12.95 each   Qty ....Total..............................

A Window on Knutsford
£12.95 each   Qty ....Total..............................

Goostrey Remembered
£9.95   Qty................Total..............................

Book Costs	£.....................................
Plus Postage	£.....................................
Total	£.....................................

Please make cheques payable to **The Silk Press** .
Please allow 14 days for delivery.